THE ASSIMILATION
OF ETHNIC GROUPS:
The Italian Case

The Assimilation of Ethnic Groups:

The Italian Case

James A. Crispino

CENTER FOR MIGRATION STUDIES
Staten Island, New York

The Center for Migration Studies is an educational non-profit institute founded in New York in 1964 to encourage and facilitate the study of sociological, demographic, historical, legislative and pastoral aspects of human migration and ethnic group relations. The opinions expressed in this work are those of the authors.

The Assimilation of Ethnic Groups: The Italian Case

First Edition

Copyright © 1980 by
The Center for Migration Studies of New York, Inc.

Center for Migration Studies
209 Flagg Place
Staten Island, New York 10304

ISBN 0-913256-39-0
Library of Congress Catalog Card Number: 80-69267
Printed in the United States of America

Preface

BY the end of the century, historians trying to make sense of the 1970s will be scratching their heads attempting to figure out why, during that decade, America believed it was experiencing an ethnic revival, a return by the grandchildren of the original immigrants (the third generation) to their ethnic heritage. To be sure, later historians will scratch their heads about many things, but the existence of an ethnic revival is distinctly disproven by James Crispino's careful and important study of Italian Americans in Bridgeport, Connecticut and its suburbs.

On the basis of a mail questionnaire that covered a wide variety of ethnic attitudes and behavior patterns, Crispino investigated the seven types of assimilation identified by Milton Gordon. His findings, based on 469 returned questionnaires and other data, show that Italian Americans are continuing to assimilate: giving up Italian cultural practices, membership in Italian formal and informal groups, and ethnocentric attitudes. In short, the straight-line theory, which proposes a decline in ethnicity with every generation in America, is upheld.

Crispino's findings are all the more significant because his study is one of the first with a sizeable sample from the third (and fourth) generation. Equally important, the sample is large enough to enable him to analyze the effects of class and religion, as well as ethnicity, on the respondents.

Consequently, Crispino paints an unusually detailed portrait of third generation Italian Americans. Most are college educated white-collar workers, professionals, or business persons, of middle or upper-middle class status, who have long ago left the Little Italies of their ancestors for the suburbs. Not only have they shed most of the remaining Italian cultural patterns they learned from the second generation, but they do not belong to Italian groups, and their close friends are neither relatives nor other Italians. The third generation chooses its groups and friends largely on the basis of class; by what people do and what interests them, rather than by their national origin.

Third-generation Italian Americans are also likely to marry non-Italians, but they do not often marry non-Catholics. Indeed, Crispino's study testifies to the continuing strength of religious ties, even if the third generation hardly accepts all of the dictates of the Vatican. His findings here are particularly interesting because Italians, unlike some other Catholic ethnic groups, came to America with a pervasive anticlerical tradition. According to Crispino's data, that tradition has not yet disappeared among the third-generation respondents, even though they, like middle-class people generally, attend church more often than their parents.

The ethnicity of the first and second generations remains alive, but Crispino shows that it has become (and perhaps always to some extent was) a working class phenomenon. As a result, third generation blue-collar workers are virtually as ethnic in behavior and attitude as blue-collar workers of the second generation; in effect, the ethnicity of blue-collar workers is as class-related as the assimilation of white-collar workers. Crispino, who is always careful not to generalize beyond his data, will not say whether blue-collar ethnicity is an effect or a cause of limited upward social mobility. Perhaps it is both, although the widespread and energetic striving for upward mobility of Crispino's respondents suggests that ethnicity now provides a significant ways of dealing with — or is a consolation for — the failure to reach middle-class status.

Ethnicity also remains alive among the middle class of the third generation, but as Crispino shows, it manifests itself largely as an awareness of, and pride in, Italian American identity. Like other students of the ethnic scene, Crispino finds that in the assimilating middle-class third-generation, a new ethnicity has developed which is voluntary rather than compulsory, and expressive rather than instrumental (I prefer to call it symbolic ethnicity, because it is expressed through and with ethnic symbols, rather than cultural practices or group memberships). New, or symbolic, ethnicity may represent the next stage in the assimilatory process, but because it is easy and pleasant to express, and does not stand in the way of further upward mobility, I believe that it may persist through at least the fourth and fifth generation.

Skeptics who remain unconvinced by Crispino's findings can, I suppose, raise three methodological questions about his study; the nature of his sample, the use of mail questionnaires, and the representativeness of Bridgeport as a study site. All three questions can be answered positively.

Crispino's sample is not random, for he was unable to identify all Italian Americans in the Bridgeport area, and thus establish the universe from which to draw a random sample. Needless to say, no one else could have done so either. Still, Crispino came close to achieving this impossible task. Not only did he devote a great deal of time to it, but he also used several methods to identify Italian Americans. In addition, he was working in a metropolitan area that he already knew well, and in an area small enough to make the task manageable. Nevertheless, Crispino rightly cautions that "generalizations based on the data can legitimately be made only to subsamples of the Italian American community, not to the Bridgeport Italian American community generally" (p. 46). In fact, because Crispino was interested in a comparative analysis across generations, he did not need a random sample; only the subsample responses were relevant.

Now that the cost of personal interviewing has skyrocketed, mail questionnaires are today a widely used research tool, and they appear to be as trustworthy as personal interviews. Indeed, questionnaires are superior in some respects because they offer more anonymity to respondents than a personal interview, and therefore, may result in more honest answers. Whatever its other virtues, the personal interview encourages respondents to supply the answers which they believe the interviewer wants or favors.

Evidently, Crispino's respondents also found the mail questionnaire interesting, for his return rate of 60 percent was unusually high. To be sure, the older and less educated were probably underrepresented both in the original sample and among those who answered the mail questionnaire, but again, Crispino's analysis focused on the subsamples, and he collected a sufficiently large subsample of such people.

Bridgeport is only one metropolitan area, of course, but its mixture of industry and commerce, of housing types and of population groups makes it typical of the kinds of Northeast and Midwest communities in which many Italian Americans live today. In fact, while Crispino properly insists that Bridgeport is not New York City, I hazard the guess that a similar study made in that city's metropolitan area would result in much the same data.

I have read many studies about Italian Americans and their communities since I wrote the *Urban Villagers* some 17 years ago, and I have been continually surprised by the similarity of the findings. Evidently, Italian Americans act and think alike, both about their Italian heritage and about their striving for upward mobility wherever they live. Perhaps Bridgeport is not typical of Italian American communities in California and the Sunbelt, where people may be more assimilated than their Eastern and Midwestern peers, although Neil Sandberg, who studied Polish Americans in California comes to roughly the same conclusions as Crispino. Consequently, I think Crispino's findings may be applied to similar subsamples of Italian Americans elsewhere and what he reports can be generalized to America as a whole.

Since Crispino's findings cast serious doubt about the existence of an ethnic revival, one can rightfully ask why so many people believe that it is taking place. Although we shall have to wait for the end-of-the-century historians for a complete answer, I want to suggest four explanations, all of which propose that some ethnic phenomena of the 1960s and 1970s were falsely thought to be indicators of a revival.

1) The 1960s were marked by an often intense political struggle in many American cities which involved, and continues to involve, ethnic residents. The mobilization of parts of black communities for greater racial and economic equality resulted in a counter-mobilization of many ethnics, notably blue-collar workers fearful of losing their jobs to blacks, and city homeowners fearing a black "invasion" of their neighborhoods. Being working-class, these ethnics were less assimilated to begin with; and because class continues to be a dirty word in American politics, the class issues which mobilized them were perceived as ethnic issues, and thus as a sign of ethnic resurgence. Nevertheless, they were class issues, so that when Mario Proccaccino ran against John Lindsay in New York City's 1968 mayoralty election, he campaigned, not as an Italian American, but as the candidate of "the little people" against the "limousine liberals". (Incidentally, the political struggle was most extreme in New York City, the source of much of the writing about the ethnic revival). Because ethnicity, like everything else, became highly politicized as a result, Crispino is right to say that "New York City is neither Bridgeport nor the nation" (p. 197).

2) the 1960s was also the decade in which the upward mobility of Italian and other Catholic ethnics became nationally visible for the first time. For one thing, their mobility culminated in the arrival of a new generation of national politicians of ethnic background — although few, if any, were elected by ethnic constituencies or because of ethnic issues. One of the first of these national politicians, Spiro Agnew, was also particularly newsworthy for other reasons, even though he changed both his name and religion before entering national politics.

Furthermore, upwardly mobile Catholic ethnic intellectuals were finally able, in the 1960s, to breach the barriers of the country's elite universities and publishing outlets. Although they had earlier lectured and written about the importance and virtues of ethnicity, their new visibility was interpreted as yet another sign of ethnic revival, and they became even more visible after the political mobilization of urban ethnics, and the political triumphs of Spiro Agnew.

3) The new, symbolic ethnicity also became visible during the same period, particularly to the mass media of news and entertainment. The national media focused primarily on middle-class America, and thus did not notice ethnics when they were predominantly working-class. In addition, the media deal more in symbol than in sociological fact; thus, they have been particularly sensitive to symbolic ethnicity. Characters like Lieutenant Colombo and Baretta appeared as heroes of popular television programs, although, like much of the audience, their ethnic behavior patterns and attitudes were minimal.

The news media reported the urban ethnic mobilization as well, and saw it as an ethnic revival. Thereafter, they also discovered the remaining Little Italies and other ethnic enclaves, treating them as bulwarks of *Gemeinschaft* against mass society *Gesellschaft*. A handful of ethnic intellectuals who held the same view of ethnicity briefly became "media personalities" in the process.

4) The new interest in ethnicity also produced many books about the immigrant culture, which was itself taken as yet another sign of an ethnic revival. While ethnic writers were celebrating this culture even as it was disappearing, there were few empirical studies of today's ethnic populations, and even fewer of people who had moved to the suburbs. As a result, the continuing assimilation of the third generation has remained virtually invisible. (Admittedly, ethnic surburbanites are scattered, hard to find, and therefore, costly to study, but Crispino, who had only a tiny amount of financial help, and used some of his own meager funds, was able to reach them. I hope, therefore, that his study will be a model for other researchers without grants, and a reminder to the private and public granting agencies that much remains to be done.)

There is a fifth explanation for the belief in an ethnic revival, which is itself an indicator of the fact that assimilation is continuing. Anthropologists have often observed the occurence of revival movements, brief and always unsuccessful attempts to resuscitate a dying culture, and I suggest that their findings apply to America as well. In other words, the intellectuals and other cultural activists who are deliberately seeking to revive the immigrant culture are, in a way, members of a revival movement — and so in a lesser way, are the people who believe that such a revival is taking place.

I should note that Crispino did not embark on his study to question the existence of the ethnic revival; nor does his book place so much emphasis on the topic as my foreword. Indeed, Crispino is more concerned with surveying the state of Italian American ethnicity in general, and he writes at length, for example, about the current nature and pace of seven types of assimilation, and about the complex, and now highly topical, relationship of ethnicity to religion and class. Crispino's book is an important work in more ways than one.

Herbert J. Gans, Columbia University and
Center for Policy Research

Acknowledgements

I am grateful to the following persons and institutions who have assisted in this study:

Professor Herbert Gans, who provided encouragement, constructive criticism and helpful advice not only during the course of the research but also throughout my career at Columbia University, where an earlier version of this work was presented as a doctoral dissertation;

The members of the defense committee — Conrad Arensberg, Allen Barton, Kenneth Jackson and Ben Zablocki — who contributed many useful comments;

Brooke Carlson, who performed the difficult task of typing the various drafts of the manuscript;

Dr. John Shurdack, Director of the Fairfield University Computer Center, and Gerald Tiano, Director of the University of Bridgeport Computer Center, who contributed the use of their facilities for the analysis of the data; Father Lawrence Kelly and Robert Bastien of these institutions provided valuable technical assistance;

The People's Savings Bank of Bridgeport and its Vice-President, Leonard Mainiero, who provided financial assistance for the typing of the dissertation;

Patricia Bruno, Phil Clark, Anthony Conte, Donna Crispino, Stella Crispino, Joseph DiMenna, Anthony DiPronio, Evelyn Dudeck, Riccardo Ferguson, Charles Framularo, John Hutchinson, Robert Laska, Anthony Petillo, Stephanie Richardson, Alphonse Senese, Stanley Siwicki, Frank Slinko, Catherine Slinko, the Sunshine Club of the Italian Community Center, Marie Tamburini and John Zielinski, each of whom made a substantial and unique contribution to the work;

George Puglisi, whose knowledge of the Italian American community in the Bridgeport area has been particularly helpful;

The 469 Italian American respondents who devoted their time to completing a questionnaire and who provided the data without which this study could not have been done;

Finally, my wife Mary Beth, and son, James, for the countless ways in which they helped to bring this work to fruition.

JAC

June, 1979

Contents

Part III

List of Tables

List of Figures

Introduction

A review of the current literature concerned with ethnicity reveals a plethora of questions and a dearth of answers with regard to the value and behavior patterns of white ethnic groups today. This is especially true with regard to the attitudes and life styles of later-generation ethnics of the new immigration — those persons arriving *en masse* in the late nineteenth and early twentieth centuries from Southern and Eastern Europe (Italians, Czechs, Poles, Hungarians). The data that do exist, derived mainly through national surveys conducted by the National Opinion Research Center at the University of Chicago [1] pertain to the demography of ethnicity — how many there are, where they live, what types of jobs they have, how they feel on public issues, etc. While fruitful as a basis upon which to compare ethnic and ethno-religious groups on a variety of background variables and civic questions, such information is found wanting when it comes to a discussion of actual behavioral patterns. Our knowledge of the life styles of later-generation ethnics remains on the intuitive level, even with the publication of a myriad of journalistic and historical accounts — some accurate, some polemical, some sentimental — of the culture and social relationships of early immigrants and the departure from such traditional patterns among their descendents.

This is not to deny, of course, that some important empirical and theoretical contributions to our understanding of ethnicity and assimilation have been made over the last several decades. Notable among those who have done work in this field are Warner and Srole

---

[1] *See,* for example, Andrew M. Greeley, *Ethnicity in the United States.* New York: John Wiley and Sons, 1974.

(1945), Gans (1962) and William Foote Whyte (1943) in the area of community studies, Michael Parenti (1967) and Raymond Wolfinger (1965) on politics, Joshua Fishman (1966) and Stanley Lieberson (1970) in the area of language, Milton Gordon (1964) and S.N. Eisenstadt (1954) on assimilation and J. Milton Yinger (1963), Will Herberg (1955) and Gerhard Lenski (1963) on religion. Others (Glazer and Moynihan, 1970; Greeley, 1969 and 1974; Abramson, 1973) have emphasized the pluralistic nature of American society, while some (Novak, 1972; Gambino, 1974; Levy and Kramer, 1972) have stressed ethnic vitality. Sound, theoretical formulations, informed by empirical research on later generational ethnic behavior, however, are conspicuous by their absence in the sociological literature.

How do white ethnics live today? What norms do they follow? What interests do they have? What kinds of life styles do they practice? Such questions, seemingly simple to answer, are unanswerable with the available data. This situation calls for a systematic, comprehensive investigation of the value and behavioral systems of contemporary ethnic groups, especially since there has been much speculation recently with regard to the character and prevalence of the "New Ethnicity". Who are those people who place flag decals on their cars, who subscribe to newly established ethnic magazines, who take trips to the "Old Country"? Are we in the midst of an ethnic resurgence or return? Is ethnicity taking on a new form in the latter part of the twentieth century? Or are we just paying increasing attention to a phenomenon which has always existed?

This book is not a study of Italian Americans in the United States. It is a study of the assimilation process as it applies to Italian Americans. Its purpose is to determine whether and to what extent the Italian ethnic group in the United States has lost its corporate identity, has become acculturated to the larger society's cultural and value systems and has assimilated into its social groupings. This work is intended to specify the areas of social life and the degree to which Italians have become less "Italian". The research is basically a study of intra-ethnic cultural and social structure, with emphasis on cultural traditions and social participation in the neighborhood, in friendship groups and in marriage partner selection.

Data on 469 Italian Americans were collected and analyzed within the framework of Milton Gordon's (1964) seven subprocesses of assimilation: cultural, social structural, identificational, marital, attitudinal and behavior receptional and civic (these terms are discussed in Chapter 3). The theoretical model is a protocol for examining patterns of assimilation and acculturation in each subarea. The straight line theory of assimilation, which is the basic assumption of this study, is that later-generational movement is correlated positively with upward social mobility and that both factors predict a decline in adherence to traditional value and behavioral forms. Thus, the methodology involves the establishment of a base-line of information against which to compare later-generation values and life styles. The perspective from which assimilation is viewed is not that of the extent to which Italian Americans become similar to other groups in America but of the degree to which they depart from a specifically Italian way of life. This study is an examination of the response of the Italian ethnic group to its assimilation experience; it is an inquiry into the characteristics of those ethnics who are more or less assimilated and into the form and prevalence which Italian American ethnicity assumes in the latter part of the twentieth century.

This book may be conveniently divided into three major parts. Chapters 1 and 2 provide the contextual framework of the study in two respects — first, a general discussion of the theoretical paradigms which have been advanced to describe ethnic behavior or to prescribe the outcome of the assimilation experience; and second, a review of the pre- and early Italian immigration experiences, which is required to comprehend the response of the first generation to the Americanization experience and to establish a basis upon which to assess assimilative movement in later generations. The middle chapters (3—10) present the study itself: from the research methods utilized to a discussion of friendship and marriage partner selection to an examination of the role of religion. The final chapters (11—12) summarize the empirical findings, place them in a theoretical perspective and discuss the character and prevalence of what has been labelled the "New Ethnicity".

Generally, the findings support the straight-line hypothesis, although there is some evidence of an ethnic resurgence in the form of increased Italian self-identity among young, later-generation ethnics. It is suggested that self-identification as an ethnic group member is increasingly encompassing the totality of ethnicity in contemporary America. Hence, the "New Ethnicity" revolves around the symbolic and intellectual needs of the individual and is characterized by being more voluntary, rational and situational than the form which predominated among early-generation immigrants. It must be pointed out, however, that assimilation and ethnicity are complex and multidimensional concepts; the more subtle aspects of these phenomena, as they are manifested among later-generation ethnics today, are only now beginning to be studied and understood. This work is a contribution to this effort and it is hoped that one consequence of its publication will be to inspire others to make inquiries into this most interesting and relevant topic.

PART I

CHAPTER 1

Perspectives on Assimilation

THE paucity of data specifically related to the cultural and behavioral patterns of later generation ethnics imposes a severe restriction on the development of theoretical explanatory models and the testing of empirical propositions derived from them. The first part of this chapter discusses early perspectives, which were ideological as well as explanatory, while the latter part examines recent paradigms more directly related to the empirical nature of the present work.

The three traditional models of assimilation are: Anglo-Conformity, Melting Pot and Cultural Pluralism.[2] Having arisen serially, each has enjoyed a temporary prominence eventually to be supplanted by another, supposedly better, explanatory model. Developing as responses to historical vicissitudes, they were more often prescriptive than descriptive of the form which the Americanization of immigrant groups would ultimately assume. From Anglo-conformity to melting pot to cultural pluralism, the perspectives increasingly recognized and accorded legitimacy to the ethnic and religious diversity of American society.

TRADITIONAL PERSPECTIVES ON ASSIMILATION

Anglo-Conformity

The central assumption of the Anglo-conformity model was the superiority and consequent desirability of preserving the English language and culture. It demanded that the immigrant renounce his cultural heritage and adapt to that which was dominant at the time of his arrival. Even though substantial numbers of Germans, Scotch-Irish, Dutch, Swedes, Swiss and Poles resided in early America, those of English descent predominated and, accordingly, it was to their behavioral pattern and value system that later arrivals were expected

[2] Milton M. Gordon, *Assimilation in American Life*. New York: Oxford University Press, 1964. Pp. 88-159.

to conform. As long as the more recent settlers did not differ too radically from those who were already present, the attainment of this goal remained a possibility.

Beginning about the time of the Irish influx in the middle of the nineteenth century, an ambivalent attitude toward immigration manifested itself. On the one hand, there was a need for newcomers to settle the West, to farm the prairies and to work in the mines and in industry. On the other hand, there was a fear of those who differed in significant respects from the white Protestant majority. The realization that "foreigners" were gaining an economic and social foothold in the New World and that no legislation existed to prevent their entrance gave rise to the Native American Movement and to the American Party of the 1830—1850 period. The advent of the Civil War submerged the ethnic issue in the national consciousness and the rapid industrial expansion which followed had a similar effect, at least for a time.

During the 1880s there occurred a significant shift in the national origins of the newcomers, from Western and Northern to Southern and Eastern Europe, and a consequent change in their characteristics and in the way in which their arrival was perceived by the "old" immigrants, i.e., English, German, Scottish, and Irish. The "new" immigrants were recruited mainly from the semi-feudal peasant, agricultural societies of Europe and tended to have little or no education or salable occupational skills. Their "odd" ways, allegedly unclean habits, poor and overcrowded housing conditions and alien conceptions of law and order were conducive to the development of an ideology which exalted the values and behavioral patterns of the "old" immigrants. Since restrictive immigration laws had not yet been enacted, the solution to the problem of what to do about these "inferior" newcomers lay in cultivating, in the mass of arrivals, a recognition of the superior ways of the host society. National, state and local units of government, public and private welfare agencies and labor groups joined in a massive campaign to educate these immigrants about the English language, the American political system and the core values of the host society. These programs were operated within a framework which, at the least, disregarded or ignored the immigrant's cultural heritage and, at the worst, denigrated his groups and institutions.[3]

The assimilative pressures increased with the onset of World War I and the "100% Americanism" movement, culminating in the demand for and eventual enactment of restrictive immigration legislation in

[3] John Higham, *Strangers in the Land: Patterns of American Nativism 1860—1925.* New York: Atheneum, 1965; Enrico Sartorio, *Social and Religious Life of Italians in America.* New Jersey: Augustus M. Kelley, 1974.

the 1920s. With the passage of a series of laws establishing national origins quotas designed to preserve the cultural and national purity of the country, the Anglo-conformity ideology lost much of its salience. This is not to deny, of course, that the major theme of the Anglo-conformity doctrine has not continued to play at least an implicit role in the continued absorption of the foreign-born and their descendants.

The Melting Pot

The melting pot ideology was implied in the Anglo-conformity model; the major difference between the two was that into which the new immigrants were melted. In the latter, it was expected that newcomers would adapt to the pre-existing culture and social structure, which was viewed as superior to anything which recent arrivals could introduce. Italians, Jews, Poles and Czechs should "melt into" the behavior and value system of the core group. The melting pot ideology took a more sympathetic view of the immigrant's heritage by assuming that it would contribute to an indigenous American type resulting from the blending of the cultures of the majority and minority groups.

Arising as a distinct ideology in the late 19th and early 20th centuries, a period when American cities were being inundated by hordes of immigrants from Eastern and Southern Europe, the melting pot ideal received its fullest expression in the works of two writers of the time. Frederick Jackson Turner (1920), an historian who introduced his thesis in 1893, emphasized the role of a changing, variegated western frontier in the creation of the American political, social and economic institutions. The challenges of the frontier created pressures for the dissolution of national groups which took part in the settlement of the West. Of course, these settlers were predominantly of English stock, so their traditions and sentiments were not all that dissimilar.

The "frontier melting pot" thesis had its counterpart in an "urban melting pot" ideology, ignored by Turner, which presented a broader view of this country's experience with immigration and assimilation. The theme was expressed in a drama by Israel Zangwill (1909) entitled *The Melting Pot*, which described the experiences of a young Jewish immigrant who fell in love with a Gentile girl. The following passage, delivered by the protagonist, illustrates the tenor and thesis of the play:

> America is God's crucible, the great Melting Pot where all the races of Europe are melting and re-forming! Here you stand, good folk, think I, when I see them at Ellis Island, here you stand in your fifty groups, with your fifty languages and histories, and your fifty

blood hatreds and rivalries. But you won't be long like that, brothers, for these are the fires of God you've come to — these are the fires of God. A fig for your feuds and vendettas! Germans and Frenchmen, Irishmen and Englishmen, Jews and Russians — into the Crucible with you all! God is making the American (p. 37).

This ideal of the "single melting pot", in its purest and highest form, leads to the inevitable dissolution of the culture and communal life of each ethnic group, since it envisions that, in some indeterminate way, a blending will occur which will produce a national whole somehow greater than the sum of its ethnic parts. A refinement of the melting pot hypothesis may be referred to as the "multiple melting pot" theory to indicate the fact that structural assimilation has occurred at a slower pace than cultural assimilation. In other words, ethnic cultures have diminished, but the close, personal relationships of immigrants have been confined largely to other members of the same group, that is, the ethnic collectivity. Ruby Jo Kennedy (1944, 1952) believes that a "triple melting pot" hypothesis is applicable to the American scene. Based on one's religious convictions, separate and distinct Protestant, Jewish and Catholic subgroups exist and there is little social assimilation across religious lines. Each religious denomination is characterized by a different rate of marriage outside the group, but this rate remains quite low, even for later generations.

Cultural Pluralism

The cultural pluralist position, envisioning as it did the preservation of the communal life, identity and culture of later immigrant groups within the context of participation in the larger economic and political system, was a concrete reality before it developed into a recognizable ideology in the early decades of the twentieth century. All ethnic groups which arrived in this country attempted to and were successful, at least for a time, in establishing distinct residential communities in which the ways of life of the Old Country could be played out. The earlier arrivals — Germans, Swedes, Norwegians — lived in sparsely settled farm areas where the enforced isolation served to create pressures for the development of a strong sense of ethnic community. Later groups settled in urban centers and participated in the burgeoning industrial economy but limited their organizational and social life to other members of their group. Within these ethnic enclaves were recreated the institutional arrangements and associational life of the Old Country: the ethnic church, the native-language newspaper, the mutual aid societies and the recreational and friendship groups. Gradually, however, these communities declined in significance and scope as later generations moved out and the standardizing influence of mass society was realized.

Special assimilative pressure, however, were aimed at the waves of new immigrants from eastern and southern Europe, who differed in significant ways from the old immigrant stock. The assault on the immigrant's self-identity, culture and social organization was instrumental in producing an ideological counterattack, led by some settlement house workers, which emphasized the worth and dignity of the immigrant and his ethnic heritage. The classic statement of the cultural pluralist position was made by Horace Kallen (1915):

> ...the United States are in the process of becoming a federal state not merely as a union of geographical and administrative unities, but also as a cooperation of cultural diversities, as a federation or commonwealth of national cultures.... Its form would be that of the federal republic, its substance a democracy of nationalities, cooperating voluntarily and autonomously through common institutions in the enterprise of self-realization through the perfection of men according to their kind. The common language of the commonwealth, the language of its great tradition, would be English, but each nationality would have for its emotional and involuntary life its own peculiar dialect or speech, its own individual and inevitable esthetic and intellectual forms (116 and 124).

We may summarize these "traditional" perspectives on assimilation by stating that each ideology embodied one major theme which attempted to answer the questions raised by the particular set of historical circumstances of the time. Because the models were not highly structured, deductive sets of propositions, the formulations of one were compatible with and tended to shade into those of another. Thus, Anglo-conformity blended into the single "melting pot" theory, a variation of which is the "multiple melting pot", which shades into cultural pluralism. Furthermore, the major themes of these ideological perspectives were presented as inevitable outcomes of the Americanization experience, equally applicable to all groups. Failing to specify how the key elements would operate in the assimilation process, they are of limited utility today in generating hypotheses regarding later-generational ethnic behavior capable of empirical testing. Now, more recent empirical models have been advanced to explain the cultural and behavioral patterns of later-generation ethnics. The theoretically divergent views on this issue may be classified into three broad categories: straight-line assimilation, the continued viability of ethnic groups as the bearers of cultural traditions and resurgence in the third and later generations.

CONTEMPORARY PERSPECTIVES ON ASSIMILATION

Straight-Line Assimilation

This perspective is based on the assumption that the cultural differences among groups become less sharp under the standardizing influence of the mass media and public education. While it is generally acknowledged that significant acculturation (adoption of host society values) of ethnic groups has occurred, there is also general agreement that assimilation (incorporation into the host society's social organization) has not kept pace.[4] The straight-line assimilation model subscribes to this notion since attitudes are more susceptible to change than are social relationships, resulting in a greater amount of acculturation than assimilation. Furthermore, the social system works in such a way that acculturation is required for mobility because of the technical and social skills needed to be successful. Moreover, most immigrants have been predisposed to accept the demands of the host society for cultural change because they found their Old World peasant cultures, bound up with the extreme poverty and deprivation of post-feudal Europe, less satisfying than that presented to them by their American hosts. First-generation immigrants, however, were less willing to abandon the ethnic communities of relatives and friends because they needed to be with others whom they could trust. Their social assimilation was also inhibited by the resistance encountered from host society members who were unwilling to permit the alien newcomers entrance into their friendship circles and social clubs.

The straight-line assimilation approach assumes that the first-generation immigrant is the most "ethnic" in terms of adherence to the traditional value and behavioral patterns of the group. Thus, the approach predicts that movement into later generations, representing increasing temporal distance from the strongest statement of ethnic culture, identity and social relationships, will erode ethnic solidarity. Generation here is of significance because it connotes temporal continuity with one's forbears, one of the determining characteristics of the ethnic group. It also serves as a surrogate for length of residence in a country, which is presumed to be highly correlated with movement into the middle and upper levels of the stratification system. Generation is important, then, because it represents the erosion of time on cultural continuity and ethnic cohesiveness and is associated with upward social mobility, which is presumed to have an independent influence on patterns of ethnic cultural and behavioral adherence.

---

[4] Erich Rosenthal. "Acculturation Without Assimilation: The Jewish Community of Chicago", *American Journal of Sociology*, 66:275-288. Nov.; Milton M. Gordon, *Assimilation in American Life*. New York: Oxford University Press, 1964. Pp. 60-68.

The theoretically important question, therefore, is the relative significance of the generation (ethnic) and the class variables, and proponents of the straight-line approach opt for the primacy of the latter. They emphasize the relative weakness of the holding power of the ethnic factor and the increasing importance of class as a determinant of values, interests and group life. Thus, as immigrants have moved into middle-class positions, in the second but mostly in the third generations, they have come into contact with similarly situated Americans of diverse ethnic, class and religious origins. Their discovery that these persons had the same values and interests as they provided further incentives for assimilation and acculturation. W. Lloyd Warner and Leo Srole (1945), supporters of this position, viewed social mobility and assimilation as a direct consequence of the length of residence in America and as the prime determinant of values and behavior. Similarly, Herbert Gans (1956) perceived a diminishing Jewish cohesiveness as Jews lost their minority status and adhered less to the formal tenets of their faith. His work on the Italians in the West End of Boston points in the same direction in its emphasis on the primacy of social class over ethnicity as the major influence on values and life styles. Gans' review of the relevant literature and empirical studies led him to conclude further that the social and cultural regularities which he observed also cut across religious lines.[5] Finally, Neil Sandberg, studying a group of Poles in Los Angeles, concluded that "...mean levels of ethnicity...tend to decline over generations".[6]

It should be noted, however, that straight-line assimilationists do not deny a place for ethnic considerations in their model. Gans (1962), in particular, is careful to note that:

> I would not want to claim that the West Enders are like all other working-class and peasant ethnic groups, or that all differences between them and other populations can be explained by class factors. Indeed, many differences between ethnic groups must be attributed to other factors in their cultural traditions and in their American experience (Pp. 241-242).

Furthermore, in as much as assimilation is viewed as a process, rather than an end result, a more proper label for the model might be straight-line assimilating, to emphasize its major thesis that later-generational movement involves upward social mobility, of which both generation and class predict a decline in adherence to the value and behavioral patterns characteristic of first-generation ethnics.

[5] Herbert Gans, *The Urban Villagers*. New York: The Free Press, 1962. Pp. 230-242.

[6] Neil Sandburg, *Ethnic Identity and Assimilation: The Polish Community*. New York: Praeger, 1973. P. 68.

Another, implicit straight-line assimilation perspective is Milton Gordon's empirical hypothesis of the ethclass, a static one, since he notes that it is applicable only to the mid-20th century United States. Mainly a blending of class and ethnicity, it is set in his consideration of a larger social reality — the subsociety. Four factors combine to form the subsociety: the ethnic group (race, religion, national origins), social class, rural or urban residence and regional residence. Gordon (1964), notes:

....The stratifications based on ethnicity are intersected at right angles by the stratifications based on social class, and the social units or blocks of bounded social space created by their intersection are contained in an urban or rural setting in a particular region of the country (p. 47).

Gordon (1964) chooses to call the social space created by the intersection of the ethnic group and social class the "ethclass" and defines it as:

....the subsociety created by the intersection of the vertical stratifications of ethnicity with the horizontal stratifications of social class.... . Thus, a person's *ethclass* might be upper-middle class white Protestant, or lower-middle class white Irish Catholic, or upper-lower class Negro Protestant, and so on (p. 51).

Within the context of a national society composed of ethclasses with subcultures, subsocieties must perform functions not carried out by either the social class or the ethnic group. Thus, the subsociety has three functional characteristics: 1) It is a source of group identification; 2) It provides a network of institutions and social groupings within which the individual may establish his primary relationships and, 3) It maintains and passes on the cultural patterns of the group. Regarding ethclass behavior, Gordon (1964) posits several hypotheses which merit full quotation because of their relevance to the present study:

With regard to cultural behavior, differences of social class are more important and decisive than differences of ethnic group. This means that people of the same social class tend to act alike and to have the same values even if they have different ethnic backgrounds. People of different social classes tend to act differently and have different values even if they have the same ethnic background...With regard to social participation in primary groups and primary relationships, people tend to confine these to their own social class segment within their own ethnic group — that is, to the ethclass (p. 52).

The Continued Viability of Ethnic Groups

A second major category of explanatory model is quantitatively, rather than qualitatively, distinct from the straight-line assimilation viewpoint. The continued-viability-of-ethnic-group approach accords greater explanatory power to ethnicity than adherents to the straight-line assimilation model are willing to concede. Peter Rossi (1964), one of the proponents of this perspective, does not accept the notion that ethnicity is nearly dead. He assigns a greater role to ethnicity, vis-à-vis class, then the assimilation approach, postulates the continuance of specific cultural traditions in later generations and emphasizes the significance of the latter in serving as the basis for the formation of political interest groups. In the public sphere — law, medicine, real estate — "rational" principles predominate; but in the private sphere of primary group attachments, men and women prefer to associate with their "own kind". Thus, ethnic groups survive and do well, as the bearers of cultural traditions, as foci for the furtherance of ethnic interests and as the "proper" sphere for establishing close associations.

From the perspective of Andrew Greeley, the urbanization and industrialization of modern society have not resulted in the replacement of *Gemeinschaft* by *Gesellschaft* but rather in the vast expansion of the latter type of human relationships. While rationality may be the rule in the "public" sphere, in private life men still prefer to be with others like themselves. Those of like religion and ethnicity provide a population pool from which the individual may choose those with whom he wishes to form intimate, trusting relationships. Ethnicity, then, is one form, among many, which can serve as a criterion available for choosing compatible others. Furthermore, "...ethnic collectivities are one of the sources available to contemporary Americans for finding self-definition, social location, and preferential role opposites".[7] Thus, far from being a divisive force, ethnicity is "...the very stuff out of which the society is created and the cement that keeps it from coming apart".[8]

Greeley does not perceive the assimilationist perspectives — Anglo-conformity, melting pot, cultural pluralism, acculturation — as being precise or broad enough to indicate the true dimensions of the American immigration experience. Moreover, the acceptance of the basic assumptions of these theories precludes the adherent from asking the kinds of questions which would yield the most fruitful answers in terms of understanding the genesis and natural history of ethnic

[7] Andrew M. Greeley, *Ethnicity in the United States.* New York: John Wiley and Sons, 1974. P. 27.
[8] *Ibid.*

groups, which are "collectivities of limited liability based on presumed common origin".[9] His ethno-genesis model is eclectic in that it borrows elements from the previously accepted perspectives and combines them into a model giving a more general and precise framework within which to study the American ethnic scene. This model assumes that host and most immigrant societies shared the broad Western cultural inheritance. Each also had certain unique features. Under the influence of education, generation and American experiences, the common culture grew larger, as the immigrants became more like the hosts and the hosts adopted some of the immigrant ways. Many of the immigrant characteristics disappeared and some persisted and became more distinctive as a response to the American challenge. Greeley (1974) remarks that the end result of this "ethnicization" process is that:

....the ethnic group has a cultural system that is a combination of traits shared with other groups and traits that are distinctive to its own group. For the ethnics, then, the mix of traits and the emphasis within the cultural system are different from those of their immigrant predecessors. They share more with the common culture than they did to begin with, but in some respects they also may be more different from the descendants of the hosts than their ancestors were from their hosts (Pp. 308-9).

It is incumbent upon the researcher operating within the ethno-genesis perspective to study the natural history of ethnic groups in America. The protocol must include at least the following: knowledge of the land of origin at the time of migration, the stratum from which the migrants came, the circumstances of migration, the economic, political and social conditions in the host country at the time of arrival, the parts of the country settled in, the occupational choice of the immigrants, the functionality or dysfunctionality of specific cultural traits, the impact of internal conflicts within the ethnic collectivity and, especially, family structure and childhood practices and the mechanisms by which ethnic culture and heritage are transmitted. While this model sets forth an agenda for observing social reality and for developing the natural history of each ethnic group, it is severely limited in its utility as the generator of an empirically testable formulation. As a virtually one-theme "theory" (the common culture grows larger) it fails to set forth determinate relationships among pertinent variables and therefore, cannot be empirically tested.

Ethnic Resurgence

[9] *Ibid.* P. 308.

Marcus L. Hansen promulgated his law of the return of the third generation:

...whenever any immigrant group reaches the third generation stage in its development a spontaneous and almost irresistable impulse arises which forces the thought of many people of different professions, different points of view to interest themselves in that one factor which they have in common — the heritage of blood (p. 497).

Nathan Glazer (1954) concurred with Hansen on the "law of the third-generation return" but insisted that it was not based on a sense of nationhood but rather on a combination of nostalgia and ideology as the basis for asserting common interest. The law of return was later incorporated into the sixth stage of Greeley's (1966) six-step model of assimilation. In describing "emerging adjustment", he states:

There is a strong interest in the cultural and artistic background of one's ethnic tradition. Trips are made to the old country, no longer to visit one's family and friends, but out of curiosity and sometimes amused compassion at how one's grandparents and great-grand-parents lived. Many elements of the ethnic traditions survive, some on the level of high culture, some in a continuation of older role expectations. The younger members of the ethnic groups, indeed, delight over these differences which they find as 'interesting' and so much fun to explain to friends and classmates of other ethnic groups (p. 35).

Daniel Bell (1975) did not postulate a return to ethnicity but perceived it as an element around which the group could unite to pursue political ends:

Ethnicity has become salient because it can combine an interest with an affective tie.... . In the competition for the values of the society to be realized politically, ethnicity can become a means of claiming place or advantage...ethnicity is best understood...as a strategic choice by individuals who, in other circumstances, would choose other group memberships as a means of gaining some power and privilege (Pp. 169 and 171).

Thus, the old cultures are seen as merely symbolic and as having the potential for serving as the basis for the articulation of group interests and the mobilization of resources to further corporate ends.[10]

Nathan Glazer's initial conceptualization of the interest group hypothesis was later expanded in a collaborative work with Daniel P. Moynihan (1970). The Glazer-Moynihan thesis has received consider-

---

[10] See, Eugene Bender and George Kagiwoda, "Hansen's Law of 'Third-Generation Return' and the Study of American Religio-Ethnic Groups", Phylon, 29:360-370. 1968. Winter.

able attention recently because of the so-called "ethnic revival" which social and political scientists have been calling attention to over the past few years. The phenomenon is of such recent vintage that the returns are not even in yet. Is the revival real in the sense of there being increased ethnic group identity and participation in ethnic social groupings and cultural activities? Or is there simply increasing interest being paid to the continuing difference which ethnicity makes in American life? Glazer and Moynihan are proponents of the former position and they cite numerous examples to support their contention that ethnicity is taking on a new dimension as a focus of economic and social interests, a shift from its historical role as the locus of language, religion, and culture. Ethnicity is no longer that which is defended but serves as a solidifying force in the furtherance of non-ethnic interests. In contrast to Greeley, they perceive little commitment among later-generation ethnics to the values and outlooks associated with their traditional cultures. Their hypothesis emphasizes the group identity and political role of ethnicity and in the "Introduction" to the second edition of *Beyond the Melting Pot* (1970) they indicate three propositions regarding its changing role:

....ethnic identities have taken over some of the task in self-definition and in definition by others that occupational identities, particularly working-class occupational identities, have generally played. The status of the worker has been downgraded; as a result, apparently, the status of being an ethnic, a member of an ethnic group, has been upgraded (xxxiv).

....international events have declined as a source of feelings of ethnic identity, except for Jews; domestic events have become more important... . This is a striking and important development — it attets to the long-lived character of ethnic identification...(xxxv-xxxvi).

....along with occupation and homeland, religion has declined as a focus of ethnic identification (xxxvi).

Since at this point in the development of their model the authors were interested in the ethnic situation in New York City, their analysis was limited to the conflicts prominent there, which they believed to be a mixture of three factors:

....interests: the defense of specific occupations, jobs, income, property; of ethnicity: the attachment to a specific group and its patterns; and of racism: the American (though not only American) dislike and fear of the racial other... (xli).

CHAPTER 2

The Immigration Experience

To understand the culture and pattern of social relationships characteristic of early generation ethnic groups, it is necessary to examine
their antecedents in the home country. This is true for Italians, as it is
for most immigrant groups, whose residential clustering represented
an attempt to retain, intact, the way of life associated with their native
land. The large number of "Little Italies" in American cities in the early
years of the twentieth century and the labeling of their residents by
one prominent sociologist as "urban villagers" attests to this fact.[11]
The desire to preserve communal life and ethnic traditions is characteristic of Italians in general but more so of those from southern than
from northern provinces, perhaps because such a large proportion
of the former left their homeland with the intention of someday
returning. Since the majority of all persons to come to the United
States from Italy during the period of mass emigration (1880—1925)
were from the south of Italy and Sicily, it is the political, social and
economic conditions of these areas which form the context of the
move and which, therefore, are of the greatest interest to us.[12]

A BRIEF POLITICAL HISTORY OF ITALY
UNTIL MASS MIGRATION

The history of Italy is the history of a "geographical expression" not a
nation, a land marked by continuous internal conflict, invasions
and political fragmentation. Even before the birth of Christ, Rome
was merely one of hundreds of city-states engaged in intense rivalry
and competition for control. The birth of Italy occurred from the
third century B.C. until the third century A.D., during which time the
Roman Empire imposed a unity on the peninsula which was not

[11] Herbert Gans, *The Urban Villager*. New York: The Free Press, 1962.

[12] *See*, Robert F. Foerster, *The Italian Emigration of Our Times*. New York: Arno
Press, 1969; Richard Schermerhorn, *These Our People*. Boston: O.C. Heath and
Company, 1949; Phyllis H. Williams, *Southern Italian Folkways in Europe and America*.
New Haven: Yale University Press, 1938.

to be seen again for another 1500 years. Under the aegis of the most advanced culture of any of the sovereign city-states, Rome extended its power and influence far beyond the boundaries of the present-day Italy. Following its fall in 476 A.D., there was a succession of foreign invasions, none of which resulted in the subjugation of all of the Roman Empire. With the political unity of the Empire at an end, **poverty, population decline and lawlessness set in and continued until 1100. It was during this period that Catholicism emerged as the** dominant religious temporal power, as numerous people spearheaded attempts to protect the populace from foreign intruders. The Church's hierarchy and organization in the face of invasions and conflicts allowed Italy to maintain a dominant position until the 14th century.

The 11th century saw the beginning of the growth of city-states, as Venice, Genoa, Florence, Pisa and Milan attained nearly total independence and became the centers of political life, banking and foreign trade. In spite of political intrigues and struggles, 1100-1400 was a brilliant era in northern and central Italy in art, literature, commerce and inventions. With the formation of a number of communes, which were associations of the leading sections of each town's population, there began the stirrings of national consciousness, at least among the economic and cultural elite.

The political situation at the outset of the 16th century was as chaotic as it had been in the previous 1,000 years. Eighty city-states were forced by tyrants and oligarchies into ten autonomous regions. Some were ruled by foreign powers, some were independent, but all, at one time or another, were engaged in war with each other. The period was characterized by a succession of hegemonies; the Spanish in the south from 1530 to 1700, the Austrian Hapsburgs in the north from 1700 to 1796 and from 1814 to 1859, the French in the north from 1796 to 1814 and the Papacy in the central portion throughout this period. Arbitrary laws, oppression, heavy taxation and conflict between the nobles and the poor were the rule.

Under the influence of the French and American revolutions and with the development of a middle class of businessmen and land-owners, the spirit of national unity, dormant since the 12th century, began to reassert itself in the early decades of the 19th century. This consciousness was manifested in a series of unsuccessful revolutions during the 1820s, 1830s and in 1848. The strain toward national unification, however, was not to be denied and the formal, political process commenced in 1859 when Cavour, the Prime Minister of Sardinia, sought a place for his territory as the spokesman for Italy against Austria. With national unity under Sardinia as his goal, Cavour organized a group of Italian patriots who commenced to wage war with Austria in 1859. With the aid of France, Cavour was able to annex almost all of northern Italy, except Venetia, down to the Papal States by 1860. In the same year, Garibaldi and his "red shirts" fought successfully against the Kingdom of Naples and acquired Sicily and southern Italy. There then remained only Venetia and Rome to be annexed for complete Italian political unification to occur. This process began in 1861 when Victor Emmanuel II, king of Sardinia, declared the formation of the Kingdom of Italy and announced the appointment of himself as its king. In 1866, King Victor Emmanuel supported Prussia in a war against Austria and as a result acquired Venetia. Rome was annexed by default in 1870 when war between France and Prussia forced the French to withdraw their troops protecting the city, permitting the Italian army to enter and complete the unification process begun 11 years earlier. With the secularization of church land in 1870, the revolution succeeded in its goal of making Italian unity a reality.

The revolution was a political, not a social one. The middle class from the northern provinces ascended to power and virtually denied the existence of the poverty-striken south as it implemented programs of economic growth, land reclamation and education, mainly in the north. Reforms in the south were slow in coming and could not undo the poverty and parochialism caused by centuries of conflict, invasions and oppression by foreign rulers.

The Agricultural Class, and Religious Systems

The description of the agricultural and class structure and religious belief system below applies mainly to southern Italy and Sicily and, to a lesser extent, to northern Italy during the period of mass emigration, from 1880—1925. The forces which were to effect the industrial development of the latter had little impact at this time on the feudal, agrarian economy of the south and were just beginning to be felt in the north.

The dominant factor which influenced all aspects of Italian life in both regions was the semi-feudal agricultural system.[13] With the formal unification of Italy during the period 1859—1870 and secularization of church lands in 1870, there occurred a limited division of large landholdings and a distribution of them amongst proprietors and peasants alike. This process followed an uneven course; despite the opportunity to effect a redistribution of land among the poor, outright fraud, exorbitant tax levies and fear of divine punishment thwarted the egalitarian movement. The result was an actual decrease

[13] Robert F. Foerster, *The Italian Emigration of Our Times*. New York: Arno Press, 1969. Pp. 65-82.

in most provinces in the number of landholders and an increase in the number of absentee proprietors and, consequently, in the numbers of tenants and day laborers. The outcome of this development was that the peasants remained poor, barely able to eke out a subsistence from the land, the large estate holders became richer and conditions conductive to mass emigration were perpetuated.

The unfavorable situation resulting from such an institutional arrangement might have been mitigated had soil and climatic conditions been suitable to agriculture. Such was not the case. In both northern and southern Italy, the topography was hilly, rain sparse and the soil infertile. The development of an irrigation system in the north increased somewhat the productivity of the land, but the small plots, dictated by the irregular terrain, and the adverse weather conditions served to hinder the technological development of farm labor and to perpetuate an un-economical system of tilling the soil.

While southern Italian farmers had little choice but to live at subsistence levels, northerners, closer geographically, culturally and socially to the remainder of Europe, developed a cosmopolitan outlook and more readily legitimated migration to improve their position. Thus, many persons from Piedmont and Lombardy became traders or migrated seasonally between their homeland and other European countries, while others moved permanently to North and South America to seek their fortunes. Prior to the mid-1880s, most Italians who emigrated to the United States were from the northern provinces. Subsequently, however, the southern Italian peasantry, driven by economic deprivation, oppressive tax burdens and backbreaking physical labor with meager returns, moved off the land en masse, some to developing industrial centers in the north and the greater part to join the urban working class in America.

The typical local community in southern Italy in the late 19th century consisted of four social classes:[14] 1) The upper class (galantuomini): nobility, large landowners, professionals and the clergy; 2) Artisans (artigiano): merchants, artisans and minor officials; 3) Farmers or peasants (contadini): persons who owned or leased small tracts of land and who thereby had a higher income and status than the day laborers; and 4) Landless day laborers (giornalieri): persons who performed on an as-needed basis, manual labor for landed proprietors and tenant farmers.

Actual landowners represented a small proportion of the agricultural

---

[14] Edward C. Banfield, *The Moral Basis of a Backward Society*. New York: The Free Press, 1958. Pp. 47-49, 69-81; Robert F. Foerster, *The Italian Emigration of Our Times*. New York: Arno Press, 1969. Pp. 85-89.

population and their holdings were diminutive and unable to produce a decent livelihood; they were subject to heavy and unequal state and provincial land, animal and building taxes and high mortgage payments. The tenant who rented a large estate was generally successful, but there were not many persons in such a position. Since the bulk of the population was *contadini* or *giornalieri*, southern Italian life was one of chronic deprivation and poverty. The peasants lived close to the land, subject to the vagaries of the weather and the changing and uncertain fortunes of the small percentage of the population which controlled their economic well-being. A brief passage from the classic work of Robert L. Foerster (1969) illustrates the harshness of these conditions:

> ....the house itself, often of only one room, may contain during the night and part of the day, not only the entire family, with a demoralizing collapse of privacy, but the ass, goat, poultry, and other animals, all making assaults upon order and cleanliness; heroic is the role of many wives in keeping their households clean. It even happens that several families will occupy one room. When the workplace is far away, the worker may remain in the fields overnight, perhaps throughout the season, resting on the ground, or perhaps on straw, with a straw roof over his head (p. 94).

The southern Italian peasant was profoundly religious (Vecoli, 1969). His religion was one in which the forces of good and evil constantly waged war for the Italian's loyalty. It thus had room for the traditional Catholic images of Christ, Mary and the patron saints as well as for the evil eye, the Black Madonna and curses. Since life was miserable, hopeless and fatalistic, it was natural to wonder who controlled one's destiny; it was much safer, therefore, to put faith in and placate both the forces of good and of evil. Thus, southern Italians were profoundly religious in the sense that they subscribed to a folk religion, the beliefs and practices of which did not conform to the doctrines and liturgy of the Catholic Church. As Sartorio (1974) has observed:

> **Italians may not keep the Sabbath day, may not go to church, but once in a whole life, may despise and reject the teachings of the Church and yet be religious (p. 79).**

Moreover, in the peasant's view, the priest was a money-grubbing hypocrite because he either came from the wealthy class or supported it. The anti-clerical attitude dated back to the period prior to 1859, when the Church owned vast tracts of land and was associated with the upper classes and the *status quo*.[15]

THE SOCIAL STRUCTURE — THE FAMILY

To understand the southern Italian social structure is to understand the southern Italian family. Leonard Covello (1967) stated:

> The concept of family that prevailed in South Italy was that of a social group which included all blood and in-law relatives up to the fourth degree. To the southern Italian, the family was an inclusive social world, of and by itself. In a *contadino* community the population consisted of a number of familial groups. There were frequent instances where one familial set-up embraced the entire population of a village; that is, all the inhabitants were related by blood or by marriage. In such a *contadino* community the social interaction actually amounted to relationships between a limited number of marriage units (p. 149).

There were two divisions in the family: one included all those related by blood and in-laws up to the fourth degree, the second was the marriage unit or nuclear family, consisting of husband, wife and offspring. Kinship ties were bound together initially by blood and affinity, later by a system of mutual protection and aid, giving rise to a pattern of social obligation having more legitimacy and permanence than law or religion. Thus, the boundaries of one's social relationships were coterminous with the boundaries of one's *famiglia*. The territorial counterpart of this arrangement was *campanilismo* (from *campana*, meaning bell and *campanile*, church tower). *Campanilismo* "...refers to a view of the world that includes reluctance to extend social, cultural, and economic contacts beyond points from which the parish or village bell could still be heard".[16] This provincialism can be traced to numerous factors, the most important of which are the narrow world view characteristic of peasant societies, the distrust of the church, which, in other societies, served as a symbol of and force for national unity, and the historically weakly unified state, which hindered the development of a strong political authority and allegiance to it. Furthermore, localism was encouraged by the hilly terrain which prevented communication from one valley to the next, resulting in isolation and town endogamy.

The limited focus of the southern Italian's interest prevented him from attaching much significance to relationships with those persons

---

[15] Bonfield, *Ibid.* Pp. 19-20.
[16] Joseph Lopreato, *Italian Americans.* New York: Random House, 1970. P. 104.

and institutions outside his immediate town or village. Gans (1962) summarizes this antipathy to outsiders in the following way:

People from other communities, even nearby ones, were characterized as criminals. The government and the police, run from Rome, were rejected with the traditional hostility felt toward northern Italy. Within the community itself, the higher classes were treated as part of the outside world because they exploited the peasants and farm laborers, and denied them any opportunity to improve their lot. Individual peasants or laborers who did manage to move to a higher social stratum were treated as renegades (p. 202).

The method which the peasant utilized to neutralize the influence of strangers (caretakers, politicians, landowners, priests) was not one of overt opposition but rather of an anti-outside world mentality. By excluding from social consideration all those beyond the kinship circle, the southern Italian peasant was able to survive in a hostile environment and to preserve his own identity. However, this attitude resulted in an inability to conceive of a larger community beyond the family and that the welfare of such a community might transcend that of the family. This led to the feeling that anyone who professed such a belief and acted upon it was not to be trusted because he was merely interested in his own personal gain, one of the tenets of the rule of "amoral familism".[17] The benefits of any action must redound to the family and all "good" ends must be achieved through the family. This method of negating external influences succeeded to a degree in Italy but was destined to be ineffectual in preserving the stability of the group when it relocated to a foreign country.

Within the southern Italian family itself, the father, whose domination was based on fear, was the absolute ruler. Family life was adult-centered; the needs of parents had primacy over those of children. The family was characterized by a strong ingroup solidarity and sharing of goals; family honor was of paramount importance. Children were considered to be an economic asset; therefore, families were large. Since most farm work was unskilled, children were prepared at an early age to work in the fields and to contribute to the family coffers. Although education was free and children were required by law to attend school until the age of fourteen, the poverty of the peasant family dictated that youngsters work in the fields as soon as they were

---

[17] Edward C. Banfield, *The Moral Basis of a Backward Society.* New York: The Free Press, 1958; Sydel Silverman, "Agricultural Organization, Social Structure and Values in Italy: Amoral Familism Reconsidered", *American Anthropologist,* 70:1-20. Feb. 1968; William Muraskin, "The Moral Basis of a Backward Sociologist: Edward Banfield; the Italians and the Italian Americans", *American Journal of Sociology,* 79:1484-1496. May, 1974.

capable of performing manual labor. As a result, illiteracy was widespread.

Marriages, which were arranged by parents, took place in the early teens between persons from the same village. The marriage ceremony was usually a religious one; no divorce was allowed and desertion was rare. For the wife, marriage represented the highest ideal. Husband-wife relationships were segregated and they were not allowed to show affection, either in public or in the family. Different sets of expectations applied to male and female: the former was expected to be tough, aggressive, to receive more formal learning than females and to be a good breadwinner; the latter was expected to raise many children, do no wage labor and be inferior and subordinate to men.

THE DEMOGRAPHY OF THE ITALIAN EMIGRATION

Based on immigration statistics kept by Italian and American authorities, the Italian emigration must be reckoned as one of the great mass movements of all times. One estimate is that a minimum of 26 million persons emigrated from Italy between 1861 and 1970, an unknown number of whom eventually returned. Since 1900 more than 10 million have departed their homeland permanently.[18] Erik Amfitheatrof (1973) remarked:

> The exodus of southern Italians from their villages at the turn of the twentieth century has no parallel in history. Out of a total population of fourteen million in the south at the time of national unification in 1860—1970, at least five million — over a third of the population — had left to seek work overseas by the outbreak of World War I ...The land literally hemorrhaged peasants (p. 138).

The trickle of Italian immigrants during the nineteenth century became a virtual torrent in 1900 when, for the first time, more than 100,000 persons arrived in the United States from Italy. Nearly 300,000 persons entered in the peak year of 1907 and approximately 280,000 in 1914. These figures represent between 20 percent and 30 percent of the total immigration to the United States during this period, up from about .25 percent in the decade 1821—1830. In 1891, the U.S. was the destination of 23.46 percent of Italian emigrants and by 1904 this percentage had risen to 67.28 percent.[19]

[18] S.F. Monticelli, "Italian Emigration: Basic Characteristics and Trends with Special Reference to Post-War Years". In *The Italian Experience in the United States*. Edited by S.M. Tomasi and M.H. Engel. Staten Island: Center for Migration Studies, 1970.

[19] G.E. DiPalma Castiglione, "Italian Immigration into the United States 1901-1904, *American Journal of Sociology*, 3:183-206. Sept. 1905.

World War I intervened to temporarily halt the exodus, which resumed after the war, only to be curtailed by the passage of the Reed-Johnson Immigration Act in 1924, which ended the century-old pattern of unrestricted entry to the United States. Subsequent legislation has been concerned with restricting both the numbers and types of immigrants permitted entry from Italy, as well as from other foreign countries. The establishment of quotas has favored immigration from northern and western Europe and of those persons with special skills from all areas. [20]

In contrast to the "old" immigrant groups — Scottish, Irish, German, English and Scandinavian — the Italians are considered part of the "new" immigration — mainly poor, unskilled persons from eastern and southern Europe. This movement coincided with the period of rapid industrialization in the United States in the late nineteenth and early twentieth centuries. As the pace of immigration accelerated, the Italians tended to become increasingly concentrated in several sections of the country: New England, the Middle-Atlantic states and the Pacific coast regions. They also favored the large, urban centers, especially New York City. The U.S. Census of 1910 classified approximately four-fifths of Italians as "urban", about twice as high a proportion as the population as a whole. Little Italies, internally differentiated by village or region of origin, mushroomed in most large cities. All Italians, however, did not live in cities; some worked in the fields as coal miners, others mined gold or became fishermen in California and nearly every state had its rural community of Italians who farmed the land.

The population movement from Italy to the United States followed the so-called "law of emigration"; the initial exodus, composed predominantly of young males seeking their fortunes, was followed by a period in which women and children, having been summoned by friends and relatives who had decided to remain, migrated in large numbers. For many immigrants the goal of emigration was to make enough money to be able to return home and live comfortably. The dream of a return to the homeland and the living out of one's remaining years in comfort was never realized for the great majority of Italians. Those who did return did so probably because they experienced economic failure in the United States, for while they came to a land where opportunities were abundant, competition for the available jobs was intense. The Italian immigrants were ill-equipped to compete

[20] For a general discussion of the new immigration and legislative action, see, "The New Immigration", *The Annals of the American Academy of Political and Social Science*, Vol. 367, Sept. 1966.

for these positions, having been farmers and farm laborers back home. A sizable proportion of the immigrants, called "birds of passage", wended their way back and forth across the Atlantic as their economic fortunes dictated. Some of these discovered that they had become too Americanized and could not readjust to the way of life of a stagnant, agricultural society. As the realization that one would not be able to return to the Old Country and live comfortably, in an economic as well as sociocultural sense, sunk in, the immigrant reluctantly accepted his status as a permanent resident.

THE FIRST GENERATION IN AMERICA

The southern Italian peasant family was surrounded in its homeland by a series of protective social circles consisting of one's immediate family, the fellow townspeople and those who lived in the surrounding region. The inner circle, composed of one's kin, was accorded the greatest amount of loyalty; if one could not find succor and aid in times of stress amongst one's relatives, he could turn to his *paesani*, his fellow townsmen, or to those who lived in the nearby territory. As one moved away from the core of kinfolk, his chances of finding material or emotional help became less certain. Beyond these circles was the outside world, a source of exploitation and deprivation: absentee landowners, government officials, and a corrupt church heirarchy.

The immigrants who arrived in this country came chiefly for one reason: to better themselves economically. In the immigrants' minds, the attainment of this goal did not entail sacrificing the closed, intimate social system which characterized their lives in the small towns and villages of Italy. The relocation to the U.S. involved the transplanting of a way of life which provided a satisfactory response to an often harsh and exploitative physical, political and social environment. In America they were received into another hostile environment. Of course, that which was deemed hostile in America differed from the threatening forces in Italy. Instead of being exploited by absentee landowners whose soil they tilled, the immigrants were taken advantage of by their employers and *padroni*.[21] Unsympathetic Irish clergy replaced the corrupt priest. The caretaking agencies were run by white Protestants, instead of by northern Italians. In the face of such adverse conditions the Italian peasant sought refuge in the only institution with which he was familiar and that he was certain could furnish him with the wherewithal to succeed in his new surroundings: his family. The kinship structure was a means of preserving one's identity and

[21] Marie Lipari, "The Padrone System", *Italy-American Monthly*, 2:4-10. April, 1935.

self-esteem, not through outright opposition to the outside world, but rather through a continuous process of ignoring its manifestations in daily living.

The immigrants' attempts to re-create the social structure of the small village resulted in a particular pattern of residential settlement: the creation in most major urban centers of Little Italies. These communities had numerous sub-communities of Calabrians, Venetians, etc., often having a street-by-street territorial basis, a collection of villages coexisting side-by-side, maintaining indifferent, sometimes hostile, relations with each other. The manners, customs, dialects, sympathies and patron saints were different within each; but always the reason for concentration was to preserve an identity and communal life against intrusion by unfamiliar and alien forces.

It should be noted that the Italian immigrants arrived in the U.S. not as "Italians" but as Calabrians, Palermans, Venetians, etc. Departing, as they were, a land torn by social and political disorganization for centuries, a state struggling to become a nation ten years after political unification, it is not surprising that the immigrant carried no national identity. Upon arrival in the United States, the *emigre* was labelled "Italian", and Italian he became by social definition, an identification which escaped him in his homeland, one of the ironies of the Italian immigration experience. The label was not all that dysfunctional for the immigrant, since it provided him with a self-definition and social location and gave him some assurance that others carrying the same label would have similar values. Furthermore, "Italian" was often equated with "inferiority" and "criminality" and this fact also served to reinforce group awareness and identity.[22] Thus, the Italian ethnic group came into being in the United States to provide support and familiarity in a rationalistic, bureaucratic urban-industrial society.[23]

Although the Italian immigration had its origin in an agricultural society, the way of life associated with this method of making a living did not conform to that which has characterized the farming community in this country. For the most part, the Italian peasant did not live in close proximity to the land which he tended. The southern Italian countryside was dotted with small, tightly compacted villages in which perhaps several thousand farmers and farm laborers and their families resided. Each dawn saw the workers trudge several miles to the fields which they owned or farmed for someone else; each sunset saw them return to their village. Thus, the emigration to America did

---

[22] John Higham, *Strangers in the Land: Patterns of American Nativism 1860-1925.* New York: Atheneum, 1965.

[23] Andrew M. Greeley, *Why Can't They Be Like Us?* New York: John Wiley and Sons, 1974. Pp. 17-18.

not entail a radical change in this mode of living. The immigrants still lived in dense, overcrowded small towns, but in tenement sections of large cities. The nature of their work did not change either; the men still left the village each day, not to work on farms, but to provide the backbreaking labor for construction projects and to fill unskilled jobs in industry.

When Italians and other "new" immigrants arrived in this country sixty to one hundred years ago, they found themselves, by reason of their status as recent arrivals, and unskilled ones at that, at the bottom of the economic ladder. Their arrival coincided with two events: a burgeoning industrial economy and the upward mobility of members of the "old" immigration. The concomitance of these occurrences created a large number of common laborer jobs in industry, public works projects and construction; the void at the bottom was filled by recent immigrants from Poland, Italy, Czechoslovakia and Hungary who dug canals and sewer lines, laid railroad tracks, mined coal and performed menial jobs in steel plants and meat packing houses. The U.S. census of 1900 indicated that 93,864 Italians, one-third of all employed Italians, were general laborers.

The first generation, isolated as it was by its self-imposed detachment from exogenous social influences, was successful in preserving for a while the most significant aspects of its group life. As the pace of immigration quickened in the early years of the twentieth century, the Italian community became a highly differentiated and relatively self-contained social system, as Italian lawyers, doctors, food stores, banks and other institutions became established.[24] Thus, the first-generation immigrant was able to participate in these types of social relationships on an intra-ethnic group basis. Ethnicity, in general, and the ethnic enclaves and communal life in particular, served as avenues of political power, markets for ethnic business, pyramids of social mobility and as psychological and cultural links between the New and the Old Worlds.

The Old World peasant pattern, subject to varied internal and external pressures, began to crack soon after its transplant to the New World. Among the forces operating to undermine the Italian way of life were: 1) the physical separation from parental authority and village culture; 2) the dependence on an uncertain wage income by the husband and the increasing acceptance of work outside the home by the wife; 3) the parent-child conflict created by the latter's greater contact with the host society in school, settlement houses and neighborhood clubs;

---

[24] John J. D'Alesandre, Occupational Trends of Italians in New York City. New York: Casa Italiana Education Bureau, Bulletin No. 8, 1935.

4) the increasing realization that the Italian way of life entailed a low social status, prejudice and discrimination; and 5) the pressures for Americanization generated by political, economic and educational institutions. The Italian family was only imperceptibly influenced by these forces in the early stages but increasingly so as the children of the immigrants, the second generation, became older and sufficiently independent to articulate their needs and desires. This phase set the stage for the transformation of the Italian peasant family to a form somewhat more akin to that characteristic of the larger society of the period.

THE SECOND GENERATION IN AMERICA

The Italian Americans of the second generation occupied a pivotal position in the processes of assimilation and acculturation. Since they were born in America, this is where their loyalties rested, in contrast to their parents, whose recollections of the Old Country, now clouded by the passage of time, were ones of fondness and affection. The diametrically opposed orientations of the generations, the first to the Old World, the second to the New, set the stage for a pattern of intra-familial conflicts having far-reaching consequences for the stability of the Italian social structure. Paul Campisi (1948) captured the essence of this phenomenon in the following passage:

....the conflict between two ways of life, the one American and the other Italian, and by the incompatibility of parents and children. This phase begins roughly during the second decade of living in America — specifically, when the children unhesitatingly express their acquired American expectations and attempt to transmit them in the family situation and when the parents in turn attempt to reinforce the pattern of the Old World peasant family. Conflicting definitions of various family situations threaten to destroy whatever stability the family had maintained through the first period...it is the parents who have the most to lose, for their complete acceptance of the American way of living means the destruction of the Old World ideal (p. 498).

The second-generation teenager of Italian descent, growing up in urban America in the 1920s and 1930s broke away, both physically and culturally, from the Italian colonies. His contacts became increasingly diversified, as he associated with classmates at school, other youths on street corners and at neighborhood centers and eventually other enlisted men in the armed forces. The result of these non-Italian contacts and of mass media messages preaching the values of American culture was increasing tension between parent and child. The psychological response of the latter to this situation was an ambivalent attitude toward the parents; affection on the one hand and hostility on the other. The cultural response was a rejection of the Old World way of life: the language, the cooking, the religious festivals and the mores. The social structural response was a decline in contact with family and an emphasis on association with others based on peer-group interests. Of course, not all second-generation teenagers responded in this manner. The range extended from the complete rejection of the Old World way of life to an orientation inward and a continuation of Italian practices and traditions.[25]

As the teenager moved into the young married adult stage of the life cycle, the typical response pattern was an accomodation between the "old" and the "new" ways of doing things and in the relationships between the generations. Numerous factors were related to this development: the dependence of the parents on their children to act as interpreters and guides in an alien world, the acculturation of the parents themselves with their understanding that success for their offspring was dependent on a disavowal of Italian culture, the establishment of separate households by the young marrieds and their realization that their participation in the American cultural ethos did not necessarily require complete repudiation of Italian group life. Thus, there was significant acculturation, a moving away from the values, customs and mores of the Italian peasant culture, accompanied by a lesser amount of assimilation, an abandonment of the highly integrated family circle.

The data that exist demonstrate that both acculturation and assimilation occur in the second generation, with the former proceeding at a somewhat more rapid rate than the latter. Based on a participant-observation study which he conducted among second-generation working class Italians in the West End of Boston in 1957—1958, Herbert Gans found that considerable change had taken place between the immigrant generation and their offspring.[26] The ethos of "amoral familism" declined in importance as competition for scarce jobs receded: one need no longer fear persons outside the family circle as a threat to one's wellbeing. Thus, neighbors and unrelated persons came to be viewed as potential friends and associates, not as competitors. Similarly, hostile attitudes towards the outside world — the law, the government, and the caretaking institutions — began to show signs of lessening as

---

[25] Irvin Child, *Italian or American*. New Haven, Yale University Press, 1943; Paul J. Campisi, "Ethnic Family Patterns: The Italian Family in the United States", *American Journal of Sociology*, 28:443-449. May, 1948; Lydio F. Tomasi, *The Italian-American Family*. Staten Island: Center for Migration Studies, 1972.

[26] Herbert Gans, *The Urban Villagers*. New York: The Free Press, 1962. Pp. 204-209.

their function and purpose became more comprehensible.

The major changes that took place between the first and second generations occurred among the children and in the increase in independence and family influence of the woman. Differing concepts of the role of the child created a division between parents and agents of socialization of the larger society, i.e. the school administrators. The former viewed their offspring as little adults and since the family was adult-centered; strict obedience was demanded. The male was considered to be an economic asset and because employment was available, he was expected to work rather than have his masculinity impaired by the educational system. Gans, citing the work of Leonard Covello,[27] suggests that the outcome of this struggle depended on the peer group; if it was predominantly Italian, truancy with parental approval was the rule; if it was non-Italian, there was a feeling of the inferiority of the parental culture and an adoption of that of the non-Italian majority.[28]

The role of the woman in southern Italian society was based on subservience and dependence on the man. She was not allowed to make a financial contribution to the family and her major purpose was to preserve her virginity so that, in an arranged marriage, she would prove to be an economic and social benefit to her family. In America, much of this changed. The dominant culture did not emphasize the subservience of the female nearly so much as the Italian peasant culture did. The woman found the female-dominated school system compatible and discovered that it could be used as an avenue of escape from a restrictive home environment; she could get a job; economic and social mobility opportunities diminished the advantages to the parents of the arranged marriage so that she was free to choose her own boyfriends and husband. However, the female was still expected to retain her virginity and marry a man of Italian descent (Gans, 1962). Gans' conclusion is that:

> American culture, however, could not penetrate the family circle. Thus, whereas the children who became the adults of the second generation retained little of the Italian culture, they did retain most of its social structure (p. 208).

THE THIRD GENERATION AND BEYOND

The major problem of the second generation was its marginal position

[27] *Ibid.* P. 206.

[28] *See also,* William Foot Whyte, *Street Corner Society*. Chicago: The University of Chicago Press, 1943.

between the Old World culture and the demands of the American system to acculturate as quickly and as completely as possible. This in-between-cultures problem was largely resolved by the time the third generation arrived. However, there still remains the empirical question of whether and to what extent the abandonment of ethnic heritage and identity and the dimunition of the ethnic factor in other areas of life continue into later generations, leading ultimately to the demise of the ethnic group as a distinct entity.

The data to help answer this question are minimal and inconclusive. Several researchers (Kennedy, 1944, 1952; Bugelski, 1961; Abramson, 1973) who have worked with data on patterns of intermarriage have demonstrated a declining rate of ingroup marriage in later generations. Abramson, using NORC data,[29] indicates that the rate of ethnic exogamous marriage for Italians increased from 29 percent for early generations (first and second) to 58 percent for later generations (third and later). He also shows that ethnic exogamy increased as higher levels of education were attained (p. 87). In a study conducted in Providence, Rhode Island, John Goering (1971) found some evidence of a resurgence in ethnic identity in those persons who belonged to the third generation. Based on his interviews with Italians and Irish, in which 70 percent of third-generation respondents, but only 50% of the first and second generation, think of themselves as ethnic and believe it important, he concluded that, at least in terms of ethnic identity, there is a return in later generations. This, however, is and attitudinal response and cannot be interpreted as a behavioral return.

To cite several examples of studies of other ethnic groups one must also note Sandberg's (1974) examination of attitudes among Polish Americans in Los Angeles toward the preservation of their ethnic and religious culture. His analysis led him to conclude that ethnicity, as measured by his group cohesiveness scale, showed a virtual straight-line decline generationally and was inversely related to class. Kramer and Leventman (1961) studying the Jewish population in Minneapolis, found a significant degree of ethnic friendship homogeneity. In the third generation, amongst which 80 percent indicated that their four closest friends were all Jews.[30] However, 70 percent of third-generation respondents, compared to 0 percent of second-generation respondents, indicated that their wider friendship group included some gentiles. The authors' conclusion was that "...Jews are increasingly stratified by the same criteria that differentiate the general community."[31] Further-

[29] Harold Abramson, *Ethnic Diversity in Catholic America*. New York: John Wiley and Sons, 1973. P. 77.

[30] Judith R. Kramer and Seymour Leventnan, *Children of the Guilded Ghetto*. New Haven: Yale University Press, 1961. Pp. 175-176.   [31] *Ibid.* P. 196.

more, "Social variation within the third generation is produced by occupational differentiation".[32] Edward O. Laumann (1973), analyzing data on 1,013 white males collected in 1966 by the Detroit Area Study, found a similar pattern. Later-generation persons were characterized by decreasing homogeneity in their religio-ethnic friendship networks. There was, however, an increase in the occupational homogeneity of these friendship groups.

[32] *Ibid*. P. 200.

PART II

CHAPTER 3

The Research Design

THE SEVEN MEASURES OF ASSIMILATION

THE theoretical framework within which this study is designed is that of Milton Gordon (1964), who postulates seven dimensions, or continua, along which the progressive movement of an ethnic group on the path to assimilation into the host society may be gauged. Each dimension is an analytically and empirically distinct element of the assimilation process. Thus, it is possible to have differential movement along the continua and to develop hypotheses concerning the relative pace of assimilative sub-processes and the primacy among them. Since each subprocess is likely to occur at a different rate, each ethnic group will have a different and unique assimilative profile, based on its standing on each of the seven measures, which are presented below:

1. Cultural Assimilation — the ethnic group changes its values and norms to those of the host society;

2. Structural Assimilation — the ethnic group takes on large-scale primary group relationships with members of the host society entering fully into the societal network of groups and institutions;

3. Marital Assimilation — members of the ethnic group intermarry with members of the host society;

4. Identification Assimilation — the sense of peoplehood based on one's ethnic group is replaced by one based on the host society;

5. Attitude Receptional Assimilation — the ethnic group encounters lesser amounts of prejudice;

6. Behavior Receptional Assimilation — the ethnic group is subject to lesser amounts of discriminatory behavior; and

7.   Civic Assimilation — the ethnic group does not raise any issues
     involving value and power conflict with the host society.[33]

This model presents a series of conceptual categories which may be
applied to empirical data, permitting an understanding of the subprocesses and the direction assimilation has or may take. In a
preliminary fashion, Gordon (1964) developed several hypotheses,
based on empirical experience to date. These may be described:

> 1) cultural assimilation, or acculturation, is likely to be the first of
> the types of assimilation to occur when a minority group arrives on
> the scene; and 2) cultural assimilation, or acculturation, of the
> minority group may take place even when none of the other types of
> assimilation occurs simultaneously or later, and this condition of
> 'acculturation only' may continue indefinitely...

Once structural assimilation has occurred, either simultaneously
with or subsequent to acculturation, all of the other types of assimilation
will naturally follow (p. 77).

The methodology utilized in this research, described more fully
below, entails the operationalization of the seven assimilative variables;
the empirical analysis involves the measurement of the degree to
which Italian Americans in the sample have departed from their
traditional cultural and behavioral patterns.

OPERATIONAL PROCEDURES

Implicit in Gordon's theoretical model and in our research based on it
is the assumption of the applicability to the American scene of the
straight-line theory of assimilation. Accordingly, our operational
procedures begin with the measurement of the value and behavioral
patterns of first-generation Italians who, it is presumed present the
strongest statement of ethnicity, and the departure from such forms in
successive generations. Thus, adherence to traditional cultural and
social structural ideals in the first generation serves as the statistical
baseline against which to assess whether and to what extent later-
generation ethnics are departing from "Italian" ways. The abandonment
of traditional values and life styles is accepted as evidence that the
assimilation process has and is occurring for contemporary Italian
Americans.

---

[33] Milton M. Gordon, *Assimilation in American Life.* New York: Oxford University
Press, 1964. P. 70.

Such a premise requires that there be an assessment of the relative significance of ethnic and class factors in "explaining" the behavior of later-generation ethnics. Because most Italian immigrants were poorly educated peasants who occupied low-level positions in the American stratification system upon their arrival, it is expected that later-generation ethnics (second, third, etc.) will be increasingly represented at the middle and upper levels of the class system and that both of these factors (later generation, higher class) will lead to departure from the traditional "Italian" way of life.

Our concern with assessing the independent influences of class and ethnicity has led us to operationalize the class variable through the measurement of the educational, occupational and income attainment of each respondent. This operational definition of class is dependent on a conceptualization of the American stratification system as "...aggregates of persons or families differing in values and behavior and forming a rank order of status levels".[34] Value and behavioral differentiation are seen as resulting predominantly from the differences in education, occupation and income characteristic of each level in the status heirarchy. Each stratum has a corresponding subculture, pattern of social relationships, life style and pride in those occupying a position ranked more or less highly in the system. Our assumption is that social class differentiation is significantly correlated with differentiation of life styles and that an understanding of the influence of the class variable is crucial to determining the role of ethnicity in the assimilation process.

TECHNIQUES OF SAMPLE SELECTION AND DATA GATHERING

The method of data gathering employed in the research was the distribution of a mail questionnaire to a sample of persons of Italian descent. The geographic universe consists of the Bridgeport, Connecticut metropolitan area, as defined by the U.S. Office of Management and Budget (1975), which includes the central city of Bridgeport and the surrounding suburbs of Stratford, Monroe, Easton, Trumbull, Fairfield, Milford and Shelton. This geographical area was selected for several reasons: the researcher's residence in it and the consequent greater likelihood of acceptance by his subjects; the presence of a large number and variety of types of persons of Italian background; and the fact that the metropolitan area is "...an integrated economic and social

[34] Dennis Wirong, "How Important is Social Class?" In, *The World of the Blue-Collar Worker*. Edited by Irving Howe, New York: Quadrangle, 1973. P. 303.

unit with a recognized urban population nucleus of substantial size".[35] Thus, a sample selected from it is likely to yield a highly differentiated group of persons in terms of both class and ethnicity.

Furthermore, the Bridgeport area may be considered "typical" in terms of the patterns of immigration and settlement of Italians in the northeastern part of the United States.[36] Most of the Italians who migrated to Bridgeport were illiterate peasants from the regions south of Rome who, upon their arrival, immediately joined the ranks of the urban working class, the members of which were filling unskilled jobs in the burgeoning industrial economy of the city. Most of the Italian immigrants settled in two sections of the city: the East Side and the "Hollow", a neighborhood located immediately to the north of the Central Business District. As in the homeland, religious attendance was a woman's affair; but more Italians attended Mass as the Catholic parishes (Holy Rosary and Saint Raphael's) became staffed by Italian priests. Numerous mutual aid societies were formed, both to provide insurance in times of illness or death and as a meeting place, mainly for males, where conversation and recreational activities might be carried out.

The selection of a random sample of respondents from the universe of members of an ethnic group presents the researcher with a unique methodological problem. The achievement of randomness presumes some knowledge of the universe from which that sample is selected. In the case of the Italians (indeed, any ethnic group), this knowledge is limited. There are no studies or surveys, on a national level, which accurately record the numbers or the characteristics of Italians. Even the U.S. Census Bureau does not report a separate figure for ethnics after the second generation, indicating that agency's implicit assumption of the melting pot ideal. The difficulty in establishing an adequate sample selection procedure is reflective of the inherent contradiction between ethnic self-identity and the assimilation process. Americanization is supposed to mean the renunciation of identification based on ethnicity. If this process has advanced to a significant degree, the group should lose its corporate identity and be indistinguishable from other collectivities and from the society as a whole. We mention this

[35] U.S. Office of Management and Budget, *Standard Metropolitan Statistical Areas.* Washington: U.S. Government Printing Office, 1975. P. iii.

[36] *See,* Humbert S. Nelli, "Italians in Urban America". In, *The Italian Experience in the United States.* Edited by S.M. Tomasi and M.H. Engel. Staten Island: Center for Migration Studies, 1970. Pp. 70—77; Enrico Sartorio, *Social and Religious Life of Italians in America.* Clifton, New Jersey; Augustus M. Kelley, 1974; Frederick O. Bushee, "Italian Immigrants in Boston". In, *A Documentary History of the Italian Americans.* Edited by Wayne Moquin. New Yoek: Praeger, 1974. Pp. 49—54.

point here because of its implications for the development of a suitable sample selection technique. If self-identity defines the ethnic group and if identification based on a "sense of peoplehood" disappears in later generations, how does one locate a group theoretically having no boundaries to distinguish it from others? Because ethnic group identity is more a state of mind than an objective, measurable characteristic, significant methodological problems are encountered. In the present study, any person whose ancestors originated in Italy and who implicitly claimed Italian descent by his participation in the study is defined as Italian.

Based on the availability of resources and on the interrelationships among key variables, it was determined that 400—500 cases would be required to permit the satisfactory analysis and testing of the major hypothesis of straight-line assimilation. A preliminary phone survey indicated that approximately 50 percent of those persons of Italian background who were queried would agree to complete a questionnaire. It was expected that once a person consented to fill out a questionnaire, he would actually do it; thus, it was anticipated that a random selection of 1,000 persons would produce 500 completed questionnaires. Based on this estimate, the latest City Directories for the towns in the Bridgeport metropolitan area were utilized to select a sample of persons with Italian-sounding surnames.[37] Each jurisdiction was allocated a quota based on the percentage of the total metropolitan population residing within its boundaries. Then, an estimate of the total number of households with Italian surnames residing in each town was derived through an analysis of the City Directory listings and the requisite number of persons for each locality, based on its quota, was selected.

During the period September—November, 1975, a telephone call was made to each individual chosen through the process described above and the purpose of the research endeavor explained. The person was asked to complete a questionnaire to be mailed to his/her residence.

---

[37] Although imperfect, such a procedure is perhaps the *only* one available for selecting a sample of Italian Americans, except for a large national survey, which would include Italians as a sub-sample. The limitations of this method are well-known: the tendency for certain groups to be under-represented in City Directory listings, such as the highly mobile, those who are poorly educated or speak only a foreign language. Likewise, the procedure for determining Italian surnames is deficient, relying as it does on the researcher's personal judgment of whether or not a name is Italian. It should be noted that 1.6% of those persons contacted indicated that they were not of Italian descent. If one assumes a similar rate of error in the other direction, that is, in not selecting names that were in fact Italian, 3.2% of the Italian American population with Italian-sounding surnames listed in the City Directories was excluded from the sample.

Approximately 583 persons responded in the affirmative; 355 question-naires were subsequently filled out and returned; 341 of these were usable, for a response rate of approximately 60 percent.

The shortcomings of the sample selection technique described above were reflected in its failure to provide a group of persons representative of all persons of Italian descent. Specifically excluded were those persons who do not have Italian-sounding surnames. Such persons fall into the following categories: males and females, whose mother was Italian but whose father was not; females of Italian descent who are married to non-Italians; persons who have changed their names. The last-mentioned group may be discounted as a source of sample bias in as much as court records and conversations with Italian community leaders show little name changing among Italian ethnics. Owing to the small number, until recently, of socially mobile Italians, the denial of one's ancestry through alteration of one's surname has not been necessary and, therefore, has not been widely practiced among Italian Americans.

Because of the inadequacies of the selection procedure and of the necessity to include the above-mentioned types of persons in the study, a method to secure a sample of these types was required. Thus, to fill the above-mentioned gaps in the sample, the following procedures were adopted: the solicitation of interested parties to participate in the study through the publication of an article in the only general circula-tion newspaper in the area and through the involvement of persons in the Italian community, both leaders and laymen, personally aware of individuals having the desired characteristics and willing to assist in the research. A total of 128 completed questionnaires were obtained through these methods, yielding a total sample size of 469.

For data analysis purposes, the two sub-samples of respondents are combined into one sample. This procedure is justified for several reasons. Comprehension and interpretation require not only a sample of adequate size but also a sample that is as representative of the universe as possible. Sub-samples of 341 and 128 are too small to fill out the cells in even a four-by-four table and thus present problems of inferring relationships through tabular analysis. Furthermore, the inadequacies of the random selection technique created gaps in the representativeness of the original sample which required closing if the relationships inferred were to be applied to the Italian American assimilation experience in general. The concerns for validity and reliability justify the combination of the two sub-samples. (*See*, Appendix B).

Before undertaking a description of the sample and of the methods of data analysis, it is necessary to mention the biases inherent in the mail questionnaire technique of data gathering. The major problem is the under-representation of certain types of persons: those with minimal reading and writing skills who would therefore be expected to have difficulty completing a questionnaire; those whose knowledge of English language idioms is limited; and those who are suspicious of requests by outsiders for information which may be considered personal. Consequently, those persons who do not have these characteristics are likely to be over-represented. Furthermore, they are likely to perceive the "right" answers and to respond accordingly. Finally, attitude studies tend to over-estimate the degree of interest and participation in ethnicity, since the expression of attitudinal support for the continuation of group values and traditions requires less effort and commitment than a similar response on the behavioral level. For these reasons, it is believed that this study underestimates the extent of assimilation of the Italian ethnic group.

DESCRIPTION OF THE SAMPLE

Table 3.1 is presented to convey a sense of the demographic profile of the sample and to permit the reader to make reasoned judgments with regard to its representativeness. Given the random and non-random selection processes adopted for the present study and the fact that the persons returning the mail questionnaire are a self-selected group, it is to be expected that under- and over-representation of certain types of persons will occur. Thus, the final sample contains nearly twice as many males as females. Ninety-four percent of the respondents are married; twenty-six percent have college degrees or beyond. Forty-six percent of the respondents who are employed are in the professional, technical, managerial or proprietorship categories. An additional twenty-one percent are clerical or sales workers. Thus, the percentage of white collar groups in the present sample is more than one-and-a-half times what it should be, based on NORC data indicating that 39 percent of Italians, nationwide, are in these occupational categories. The same skewness is evident in the distribution along the education continuum. It should be noted, however, that the NORC data were gathered mainly in the 1960s and do not reflect recent mobility patterns of Italian Americans.

The problems inherent in the sample selection process mean that data for the entire sample are biased. Consequently, generalizations based on the data can legitimately be made only to sub-samples of the Italian American population studied, not to the Bridgeport Italian

Table 3.1

Demography of the Combined Sample of Returned Questionnaires
Compared to National Distribution of Italian Americans

	Percent of Total In Combined Sample[a]	Percent of National Sample of Italian Americans[b]
SEX		
Male	64%	48%
Female	36	52
	100%	100%
	(N=469)	(N=346)
MARITAL STATUS		
Married	94%	82%
Separated	1	2
Widowed	2	8
Never Married	3	8
	100%	100%
	(N=469)	(N=346)
GENERATION		
First	6%	8%
Second	65	76
Third	29	16
	100%	100%
	(N=466)	(N=331)
PARENTAGE		
Both Parents Italian	85%	93%
One Parent Italian	15	7
	100%	100%
	(N=464)	(N=336)
OCCUPATION		
Professional, Technical	25%	15%
Managers, Proprietors	21	12
Sales Workers	6	4
Clerical Workers	15	8
Craftsmen, Foremen	13	24
Operatives, Unskilled	10	20
Laborers	2	3
Farm and Farm Workers	0	1
Service Workers	8	13
	100%	100%
	(N=399)	(N=346)

TABLE 3.1 (continued)

Demography of the Combined Sample of Returned Questionnaires
Compared to National Distribution of Italian Americans

	Percent Total In Combined Sample[a]	Percent of National Sample of Italian Americans[b]
EDUCATION		
Grammar School or Less	7%	23%
Some High School	13	23
High School Graduate	39	36
Some College	15	11
College Graduate	13	6
Graduate School	13	1
	100%	100%
	(N=461)	(N=346)

NOTES:

[a] The percentages in the "% of Total in Combined Sample" column are the percentages of the total number of *employed* persons in the sample. Seventy respondents are excluded and may be classified as "other" (housewives, retired).

[b] These data are based on national surveys conducted by the National Opinion Research Center at the University of Chicago: the percentages apply to the persons in the survey who indicated that Italy was the homeland of their ancestors. The data pertaining to sex, marital status, education and occupation are based on a composite of seven national surveys conducted between 1963 and 1972 (Greeley, 1974: 34-62). The data pertaining to generation and parentage are based on the 1964 NORC survey and are reported in Abramson (1973 : 26 and 53, respectively).

American population in its entirety. Thus, we cannot say that 25 percent of the Italian American population in Bridgeport have technical or professional occupations, but we can say that those Italian Americans who have technical or professional occupations exhibit such-and-such a behavioral pattern.

A NOTE ON COLINEARITY

Since the bulk of the Italian immigration to the United States occurred during a relatively brief period (1885—1925), sufficient time has not elapsed to produce a highly diversified, generationally speaking, Italian American population. Furthermore, most immigrants came from southern Italy and tended, therefore, to have similar background characteristics: they were young, had little or no education and low occupational skills. Given these two factors, the population of Americans of Italian descent is less differentiated than it would otherwise be. For example, certain background characteristics are highly associated with each other, such as age and generation (later-generation Italians are generally younger than earlier-generation Italians). There are several such relationships which are of particular significance to the present research endeavor; they must be made explicit if the analysis is not to be confounded by their colinearity and if their effect on the assimilation variables is to be properly understood.

Table 3.2 presents the distribution of respondents across the values of the background variables at each generational stage. Several of the more significant relationships in this table may be summarized as follows:

1. Later-generation ethnics are younger than their earlier generation counterparts; 74 percent of the respondents in the first generation are 50 years of age or older, while 70 percent of those persons in the third generation or later are 39 years of age or younger;

2. Later-generation Italian Americans have less Italian parentage; 100 percent of those persons born in Italy have two Italian parents, whereas one-third of those who have one or more grandparents born in the U.S. have a similar degree of Italian ethnic parentage;

3. Later-generation Italians tend to be more highly educated; 20 percent of those born in Italy, compared to 40 percent of those who have one or more grandparents born in this country, are at least college graduates;

4. Early-generation Italian Americans tend to have "working class" occupations (57% of the first generation and 40% of the second generation have blue-collar jobs); conversely, later-generation ethnics have a greater tendency to have "white-collar" positions (50% of those persons in the third generation or later are in the managerial or professional classification).

Thus, the overall relationship among the major background characteristics is one of colinearity. Later-generation persons are younger, more highly educated and less ethnic in terms of parentage than older-generation Italians. While these relationships are indicative of societal trends, they also reflect the effect of length of residence in this country in producing a pattern of Italian American upward social mobility.

TECHNIQUES OF DATA ANALYSIS

In addition to tabular analysis, Kendall's Tau is the other technique of data analysis utilized in this study. This measure summarizes the

TABLE 3.2

Generation by Background Characteristics

Background Characteristics	R born in Italy	R born in U.S. 2 parents born in Italy	R and 1 pt. born in U.S.	R and 2 pts. born in U.S.	R and 1+ grandparents born in U.S.
AGE					
60 + years	44%	28%	4%	1%	5%
50—59	30	39	27	1	3
40—49	7	23	40	28	22
30—39	11	8	22	42	37
20—29	8	2	7	28	33
	100% (27)	100% (208)	100% (95)	100% (96)	100% (40)
PARENTAGE					
2 Parents Italian	100%	99%	81%	75%	33%
1 Parent Italian	0	1	19	25	67
	100% (27)	100% (206)	100% (95)	100% (95)	100% (40)
EDUCATION					
0—8 Grades	20%	11%	2%	2%	0%
9—11 Grades	12	20	13	5	3
H.S. Graduate	32	38	44	42	27
13—15 Grades	16	16	9	14	30
College Graduate	8	8	15	22	15
16+ Grades	12	7	17	15	25
	100% (25)	100% (205)	100%	100% (94)	100% (40)

TABLE 3.2 (continued)
Generation by Background Characteristics

Background Characteristics	R born in Italy	R born in U.S. 2 parents born in Italy	R and 1 pt. born in U.S.	R and 2 pts. born in U.S.	R and 1+ grandparents born in U.S.
OCCUPATION					
Unskilled Blue Collar	35%	25%	15%	15%	8%
Skilled Blue Collar	22	15	10	10	10
Sales, Clerical	17	22	24	21	24
Proprietors	9	8	7	4	8
Managers, Administrators	9	12	17	16	11
Professional, Technical	8	18	27	34	39
	100% (23)	100% (169)	100% (81)	100% (88)	100% (38)
INCOME					
Less than $10,000/year	20%	13%	9%	6%	11%
$10,000 — $17,499/year	36	37	42	34	38
$17,500 — $24,999/year	28	29	27	36	19
$25,000+/year	16	21	22	24	32
	100% (25)	100% (180)	100% (91)	100% (90)	100% (37)

relationship between two ordinal-level variables by comparing pairs of cases to determine if their relative ordering on one variable is the same as their relative ordering on a second variable. Each instance in which the ordering of the pair of cases on the variables is the same contributes +1 to the measure; conversely, each instance in which the ordering of the pair of cases on the variables is in the opposite direction contributes −1 to the calculation. The formula used to compute Tau also takes into account those instances in which the pairs of cases are tied in their rankings on the two variables.[38] Thus, Kendall's Tau is a measure of the degree to which pairs in the "proper" order exceed those in the reverse order and ranges from +1 to −1. If every pair of cases were in the "proper" order, the value of Tau would be +1; if every pair of cases were in the reverse order, the value of Tau would be −1. If there is no relationship between the variables, the value of Tau is close to zero.[39] As an explication of the manner in which Kendall's Tau enters into the analysis. Figure 3.I presents approximately the same set of relationships as Table 3.2.

FIGURE 3.I

Interrelationships of Explanatory Variables

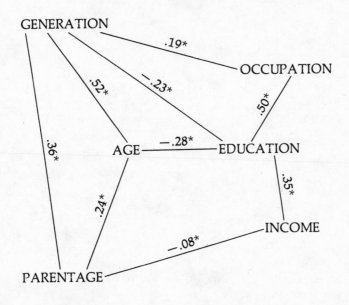

NOTE: * Significant at .05 level.

[38] Norman Nie, *et al, Statistical Package for the Social Sciences.* New York: McGraw-Hill, 1975. Pp. 227−228.

[39] Hubert Blalock, *Social Statistics.* New York: McGraw-Hill, 1972. Pp. 418−427.

In addition, another concept, that of "significance level", is introduced
Level of significance refers not to the degree of association but rather
to the probability of association. Therefore, by accepting the .05 level
of significance in this study, we are saying that there are five chances
in one hundred that the observed relationship between two variables
could have occurred by chance. That is, there is a 95 percent probability
that the same relationship would have occurred if another sample,
employing the same tecniques described above, were drawn. Of course,
the significance level is also applicable to relationships presented in
the cross-tabulation format. For the sake of brevity and clarity, any
Tau measurement significant at the .05 level which is reported in the
text will carry an asterisk (*) beside it.

The two techniques of data analysis introduced here will be utilized
throughout the analysis pertaining to the subprocesses of the assimilation of Italian Americans. Each has its advantages: Tau is a convenient
means of summarizing a relationship or of comparing a series of
relationships, without being encumbered by a great amount of detail.
Cross-tabulations permit greater specificity in interpretation of data
and allow a fuller understanding of the more subtle aspects of the
assimilation process.

CHAPTER 4

Cultural Assimilation

CULTURE may be defined as:

....the way of life of a society, and if analyzed further is seen to consist of prescribed ways of behaving or norms of conduct, beliefs, values and skills, along with the behavioral patterns and uniformities based on these categories — all this we call 'non-material culture' — plus, in an extension of the term the artifacts created by these skills and values, which we call 'material culture'.[40]

Culture is distinct from social structure in that the latter refers to:

....the set of crystallized social relationships which its (society's) members have with each other and which places them in groups, large or small, permanent or temporary, formally organized or unorganized, and which relates them to the major institutional activities of the society, such as economic and occupational life, religion, marriage and the family, education, government, and recreation.[41]

While analytically distinct, in the real world social structure and culture are always in a state of dynamic equilibrium, for it is the values and norms of society which determine for the most part its occupational structure, class groupings and social relationships, and the actions of individuals in social interaction which maintain and modify the society's material and non-material heritage. However, it is imperative that the distinction between the two be observed in ethnic group research because of the prevailing opinion that the Americanization process has involved much acculturation and a lesser amount of assimilation. If culture is conceived as the group's response to its social and physical environment, change in the latter necessarily involves acculturation, that is, transformation of the group's traditional way of doing things in response to a new set of stimuli. The process of assimilation as

---

[40] Milton M. Gordon, *Assimilation in American Life.* New York: Oxford University Press, 1964. Pp. 32-33.

[41] *Ibid.* Pp. 30-31.

incorporation into the group structure of the host society, is a different though related phenomenon and must be analyzed separately.

Migrants from one area to another bring with them many pieces of cultural baggage, such as dress, patterns of emotional expression, political style and religious perspective. The culture is essential in the newcomer's attempts to interpret and understand his new surroundings. As time goes by, alterations are made as adaptions to changing contexts are necessitated. Because cultural assimilation is a multi-faceted process, one would expect varying rates of assimilation among the several subareas and among particular groups. In this study, five areas of cultural behavior are examined: 1) Maintenance of food and language patterns; 2) Traditionalism — control over destiny and distrust of others; 3) Heritage — attitudes toward the preservation of Italian traditions; 4) Nationality — pride in Italian ancestry; and 5) Religious — attitudes toward the preservation of Italian religious culture.

MAINTENANCE OF FOOD AND LANGUAGE PATTERNS

Table 4.1 was constructed through the utilization of responses to questions concerning the maintenance of the Italian culinary style and language skills. To be sure, the fact that one cooks Italian does not necessarily make him Italian, since food habits, being one part of a group's extrinsic culture,[42] tend to persist longer than any other form of culture, as the top row of Table 4.1 indicates. It is also a pattern which, because it does not signify acceptance of the intrinsic culture of the group, is easily accepted by members of other groups in American society. When it comes to the frequency with which one cooks Italian dishes (Row 2, Table 4.1), there is evidence of declining adherence to the traditional culture. Likewise, making one's own pasta, a more discriminating test of Italianness than cooking habits in general, exhibits a similar pattern. While 44% of first-generation respondents carry on this tradition, only 15% of those with one or more grandparents born in this country do likewise, indicating the loss of a traditional culinary skill and, in a larger and more significant sense, a departure from one aspect of the ethnic culture. A similar pattern emerges from an analysis of the extent of the maintenance of language skills. The bottom two rows in Table 4.1 indicate a linear decline in the ability to read and speak one's ancestral language. Overall, there is a straight-line decline, generationally, in the maintenance of Italian food and language patterns.

---

[42] *Ibid.* P. 79.

TABLE 4.1

Maintenance of Food and Language Patterns by Generation [a]

ITEM	R born in Italy	R born in U.S. 2 parents born in Italy	R and 1 pt. born in U.S.	R and 2 pts. born in U.S.	R and 1+ grandparents born in U.S.
1. Cooks 3 or more Italian dishes.	46%[b] (13)	67% (153)	65% (69)	68% (71)	52% (29)
2. Cooks Italian dishes 3 times per week or more.	60 (20)	38 (175)	22 (85)	23 (86)	21 (33)
3. Makes own pasta.	44 (27)	32 (206)	23 (94)	25 (96)	15 (40)
4. Speaks Italian.	100 (27)	72 (208)	33 (93)	14 (95)	10 (40)
5. Reads Italian.[c]	92 (26)	33 (206)	16 (95)	5 (92)	13 (39)

NOTES:

[a] All relationships between generation and measures of maintenance of cooking and language skills are significant at .05 level.

[b] Numbers in parentheses are base N's for the percentages. Thus 46% of the 13 respondents born in Italy cook 3 or more Italian dishes.

[c] The actual questions are:
1. Do you or your spouse cook Italian dishes, besides spaghetti or pizza? Which ones?
2. How often do you have any kind of Italian dish at home?
3. Do you make your own pasta?
4. Do you speak Italian?
5. Do you read Italian?

The above findings are confirmed when the individual variables are combined into a scale, which is constructed by summing the recoded values (so that all variables contribute equally to the scale) of the five measures of maintenance of Italian language and cooking skills. Dichotomizing the values of the scale divides it into a "high" and a "low" adherence-to-ethnic-tradition group. Figure 4.I illustrates, across the values of each background variable, the percentages in the "high" category. The data indicate a straight-line assimilation pattern across the ethnic variables, generation and parentage. The crucial factor in preservation revolves around whether or not one's parent(s) were born in the United States. For the first and second generations (R born in Italy and both parents born in Italy, respectively), there is a high rate of traditionalism, 66 percent and 61 percent. For those respondents who have one or both parents born in the United States, the corresponding figures are 32 percent and 18 percent, indicating the significance for the maintenance of these skills of having parents who have been raised in the cultural setting of the homeland. The relationship between the class variables and the scale is somewhat different. There is a straight-line movement away from the maintenance of ethnic habits at higher class levels, until the highest levels of class (education, occupation, income), where there is evidence of a reversal of this trend. We shall reserve further discussion of this phenomenon until the final section of this chapter.

TRADITIONALISM

The two sets of variables to be discussed under the heading of traditionalism are distrust of others and control over destiny. Peasant societies in general are characterized by suspicious attitudes toward outsiders and by a belief that one's destiny is in the hands of fate. The extent to which present-day Italian Americans have shed these vestiges of the past is the subject matter of this section (*See*, Chapter 2 for a more detailed discussion of these traditional aspects of the Italian culture).

Distrust of Others

The operationalizing of "distrust of others" involves two questions: one pertaining to the person's attitudes toward new neighbors and the other concerning generalized mistrust of others. Regarding the first,[43]

---

[43] The actual question is: In general, which of the following attitudes do you think a person should take toward new neighbors? Check one.

FIGURE 4.I

Scale of Maintenance of
Language and Cooking Skills
by Background Variables a

GENERATION*

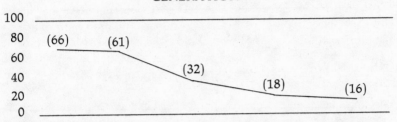

AGE*

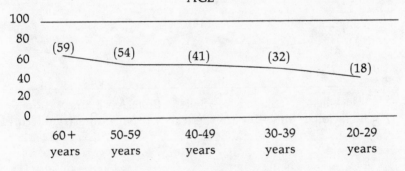

PARENTAGE*

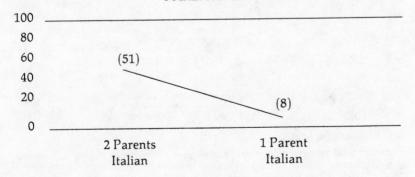

FIGURE 4.I (continued)

Scale of Maintenance of   Language and Cooking Skills
by Background Variables[a]

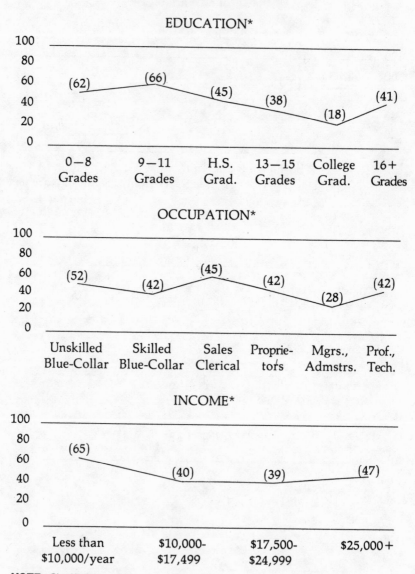

EDUCATION*

(62)	(66)	(45)	(38)	(18)	(41)
0–8 Grades	9–11 Grades	H.S. Grad.	13–15 Grades	College Grad.	16+ Grades

OCCUPATION*

(52)	(42)	(45)	(42)	(28)	(42)
Unskilled Blue-Collar	Skilled Blue-Collar	Sales Clerical	Proprie-tors	Mgrs., Admstrs.	Prof., Tech.

INCOME*

(65)	(40)	(39)	(47)
Less than $10,000/year	$10,000-$17,499	$17,500-$24,999	$25,000+

NOTE: Significant at .05 level.

[a] The figures in parentheses are the percentage of respondents scoring high on the scale.

52 percent of the respondents indicated that they would take the initiative in welcoming newcomers' to their neighborhood; the remainder maintained the attitude that, at least initially, there should be some social distance between them and the new arrivals. Regarding the concept of generalized mistrust, 18 percent agreed with the statement that "Most people can't be trusted and if you don't watch out they will take advantage of you".

The evidence to support the hypothesis of straight-line assimilation is consistent, in as much as all Tau measurements between the background variables and the measures of distrust of others, although relatively weak, are in the expected direction. Thus, the less "ethnic" one is (later-generation, one Italian parent), the less distrustful he tends to be. Conversely, the higher one ranks on the education, occupation and income variables, the less he tends to have negative attitudes toward new neighbors and to mistrust others. Thus, both higher class standing and less ethnicity predict a decline in adherence to this cultural trait (See, Appendix Table C.1).

Fatalism

The two questions pertaining to control over fate have been combined to form a destiny scale;[44] analysis of the Tau measurements indicates that the best predictors of an individual's belief in his ability to control his own future are education (Tau $= .34^*$) and occupation (Tau $= .29$). In contrast, the Tau for generation is $.18^*$ and for parentage, $.07^*$. The fatalism which is characteristic of peasant cultures is the reverse of the world view required by socially mobile persons and appears to be readily abandoned by those moving into the middle and higher levels of the stratification system. However, a slightly different interpretation may be derived through an examination of the relationships between the background variables and the destiny scale,

---

____ Go over to their house after they move in and offer help.

____ Go over to their house and introduce yourself, but do not offer help unless they ask for it.

____ Don't go over unless invited, but be friendly.

____ Don't become too friendly until you have had some time to see what kind of people they are.

____ Stay away from all newcomers and keep to lifetime friends.

[44] Each respondent was asked to indicate the degree to which he agreed or disagreed with the following statements.

We fool ourselves if we think we can control the course of our own lives.

Planning only makes a person unhappy, since your plans hardly ever work out anyway.

constructed in the same manner as that described earlier for the scale of cooking and language skill maintenance. These relationships are depicted in Figure 4.II. Although the Tau measurements seem to indicate the superiority of class over ethnicity as "explaining" one's perception of his ability to control his destiny, the latter seems to possess a holding power of its own. This observation is based on the fact that for the "lowest" values of generation (one or more grandparents born in the United States) and parentage (one Italian parent), 47 percent of the respondents rate high on the destiny scale (exhibit a high degree of fatalism); the comparable figures for the "lowest" values of the class variables are 34 percent for education and 35 percent for occupation. Thus, while a higher class standing tends to give one confidence in his ability to control his fate, ethnicity tends to diminish this belief. The overall realtionship is one in which a relatively high level of resignation to fate is maintained across generations, although at decreasing levels for later generations. Education reduces this form of traditionalism, but the ethnic factor continues to manifest itself, even at very high levels of educational and occupational achievement. The final section of this chapter contains a more comprehensive treatment of this relationship.

PRESERVATION OF CULTURAL HERITAGE

Under the heading of cultural heritage are placed those variables which assess the respondent's perception of the desirability of preserving the ethnic group's legacy. The frequency distribution for the eight cultural heritage questions is presented in Appendix Table C.2. Generally, there is some support for the maintenance of the Italian ethnic group's cultural inheritance, as evidenced by the high percentages contained in the first three columns of the table (Strongly Agree to Mildly Agree). It should be noted, however, that the majority of those who agree with any statement are contained in the "Agree" or "Mildly Agree" categories, not a very strong pronouncement of support for the preservation of Italian cultural heritage. For the purpose of analyzing the relative explanatory power of the class and ethnic variables, the eight responses have been coded into a heritage scale, following the same procedure employed in the construction of earlier scales. These relationships are depicted in Figure 4.III.

As in the case of the maintenance of language and cooking skills scale, there is a decrease in adherence to ethnic culture as one proceeds from earlier to later generations and from lower to higher class standing. The decline is especially precipitous between the first (R born in Italy) and the second (R born in USA) generations and between the latter

FIGURE 4.II

Destiny Scale
by Background Variables[a]

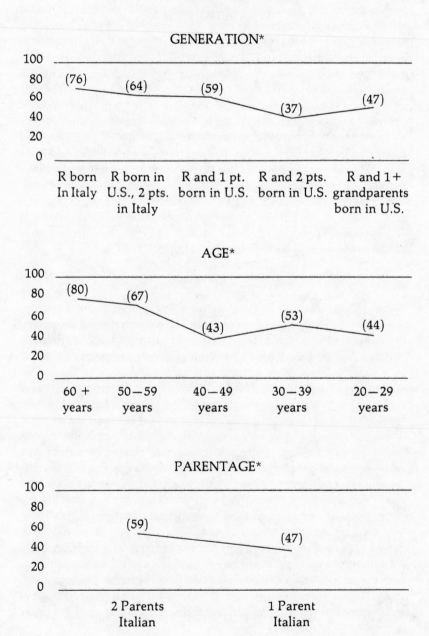

GENERATION*

(76) (64) (59) (37) (47)	

R born   R born in   R and 1 pt.   R and 2 pts.   R and 1+
In Italy   U.S., 2 pts. born in U.S.   born in U.S.   grandparents
            in Italy   born in U.S.

AGE*

(80) (67) (43) (53) (44)

60 +   50—59   40—49   30—39   20—29
years   years   years   years   years

PARENTAGE*

(59)   (47)

2 Parents   1 Parent
Italian   Italian

FIGURE 4.II (continued)

Destiny Scale
by Background Variables[a]

EDUCATION*

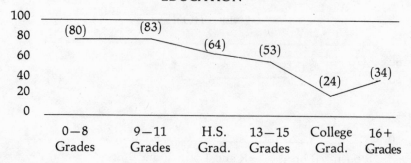

OCCUPATION*

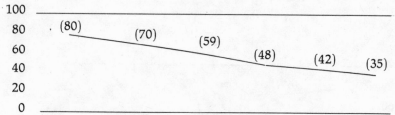

INCOME*

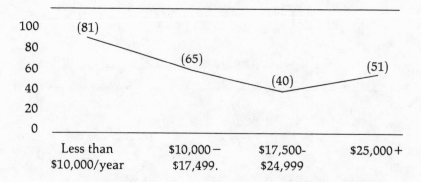

NOTES: * significant at .05 level.

[a]The figures in parentheses are the percentages of respondents scoring high on the scale (high degree of resignation to fate).

FIGURE 4.III

Preservation of Cultural Heritage Scale
by Background Variables[a]

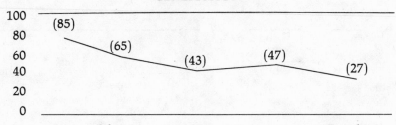

GENERATION*

(85)	(65)	(43)	(47)	(27)

| R born in Italy | R born in U.S., 2 pts. In Italy | R and 1 pt. born in U.S. | R and 2 pts. born in U.S. | R and 1+ grandparents born in U.S. |

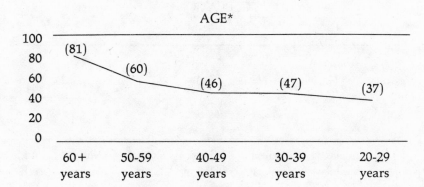

AGE*

(81)	(60)	(46)	(47)	(37)

| 60+ years | 50-59 years | 40-49 years | 30-39 years | 20-29 years |

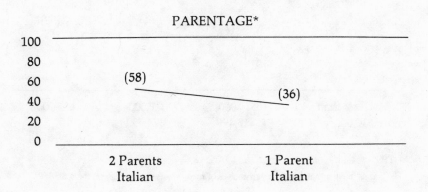

PARENTAGE*

(58)	(36)

| 2 Parents Italian | 1 Parent Italian |

FIGURE 4.III (continued)

Preservation of Cultural Heritage Scale
by Background Variables[a]

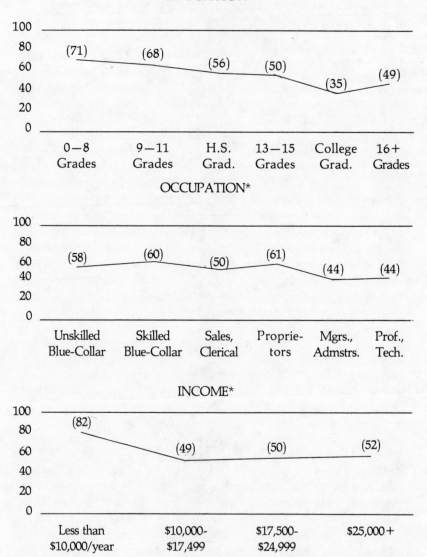

EDUCATION*

OCCUPATION*

INCOME*

NOTES: * significant at .05 level.

[a]The figures in parentheses are the percentages of respondents scoring high on the scale.

and the beginning of the third generation (One parent born in the USA). Then there is a levelling off until the beginning of the fourth generation, when again there is a steep decline in attitudes which favor keeping alive the cultural heritage. There is also evidence of an upswing in one's interest in his ethnic roots, not in the third generation, but in the upper-income, highly educated groups.

NATIONALITY

The term "nationality" is used in the present context to indicate pride in belonging to the ethnic group. Nationality is the sense of peoplehood, presumed common descent and consciousness of kind. It involves at least vicarious involvement in the fortunes of one's people; when a part of the group or any individual is under attack, the integrity of the whole is called into question. We are concerned with nationality because of its importance as an indicator of ethnic solidarity today.

This study has utilized ten questions to assess the significance of nationality in the lives of contemporary Italian Americans. The frequency distribution for the responses is presented in Table 4.2.

An examination of the distributions reveals that there are a number of specific themes contained within the generic concept of nationality. One, which has structural implications, concerns social relations with other Italians (Questions, # 2 and # 4) and indicates weak support for the strong Italian position. Half the number of respondents did not believe that an Italian neighborhood is a friendlier place to live and the majority (57%) did not feel more comfortable with Italians. Question One, with only 31 percent expressing agreement with the position that organizations are needed to express the views of Italian Americans, is non-supportive of the interest group hypothesis as espoused by Glazer and Moynihan. It is also reflective of the traditional Italian antipathy to formal organizational involvement. Questions Seven and Ten are indicative of the distrust of politicians of any kind prevalent among Americans at the same time that the survey was taken and are also testimony to the "typical" Italian hostility toward those involved in politics. Taken as a whole, Questions One, Seven and Ten are symptomatic of the persistence of attitudes, in terms of suspicion of the organized (non-Italian) community, among comtemporary Italian Americans.

The two questions which present the strongest statements pertaining to nationality, changing one's name so that it sounds less Italian and depending on other Italians to help in times of trouble, elicited the greatest amount of support from the respondents. Changing one's

TABLE 4.2

Distribution of Responses to Nationality Statements[a]

ITEM	Strongly Agree	Agree	Mildly Agree	Mildly Disagree	Disagree	Strongly Disagree	Total (N)
1. Need organizations to express Italian point of view.	3%	16%	12%	20%	41%	8%	100% (448)
2. Italian neighborhood is a friendlier place to live.	8	19	22	15	31	5	100% (450)
3. It is not alright to change name to sound less Italian.	45	38	6	3	4	4	100% (456)
4. I feel more comfortable with Italians.	8	16	19	15	35	7	100% (455)
5. Italian jokes bother me.	7	10	14	11	42	16	100% (451)
6. Can count on Italians to help in time of need.	17	45	20	7	8	3	100% (449)

Table 4.2 (continued)

Distribution of Responses to Nationality Statements[a]

ITEM	Strongly Agree	Agree	Mildly Agree	Mildly Disagree	Disagree	Strongly Disagree	Total (N)
7. Would vote for Italian politician because he is Italian.	3%	4%	4%	7%	45%	37%	100% (453)
8. Can be good Italian and good American.	15	29	16	12	20	8	100% (448)
9. Important to aid new Italians in this country.	10	29	26	12	18	5	100% (446)
10. Can trust Italian politicians.[b]	9	11	6	12	45	17	100% (446)

TABLE 4.2 NOTES

NOTES:

a These statements are based on similar ones used by Sandberg (1974) in the construction of his group cohesiveness scale.

b The actual statements are:

1. We don't need stronger organizations to express the views of Italian Americans. (Note that this statement has been reworded in the table so that all "agree" responses represent support for the Italian position.)

2. An Italian neighborhood is a friendlier place to live.

3. It is alright to change your name so that it will not be taken for Italian. (*See,* note for Statement #1 above.)

4. I feel more comfortable with Italian people.

5. Italian jokes bother me.

6. If you're in trouble, you cannot count on Italian people to help you. (*See,* note for Statement #1 above.)

7. I would vote for an Italian political candidate rather than any other nationality regardless of political party.

8. You can be for your own people first and still be a good American.

9. It is important for me to help Italians who have just come over from Italy to adapt to the American way of life.

10. Italian politicians can't be trusted any more than other politicians can. (*See,* Statement #1 above.)

name is, in a sense, betraying one's family and people; it is a rejection of the group, a threat to its survival and, as such, is resisted vehemently. Similarly, if one cannot depend on others like oneself (ethnically speaking) to help in time of need, then the foundations of the group are weak and its continued viability is problematic. In this regard, it is interesting to note that, while 82 percent of the respondents believed that they could count on other Italians to help in time of need, 65 percent agreed that it was important to help new Italians in this country. Thus, Italian Americans in the sample appear more often to want help than they would be willing to give it.

The scale construction technique developed earlier was employed to build a nationality scale, composed of these ten questions. That declining ethnicity is associated with later-generational movement is indicated by the slope of the generation, parentage and age lines (Figure 4.IV). The same curvilinear relationship observed earlier between traditionalism and class also obtains in the present instance. While there is a straight-line generational departure from ethnic cultural patterns, class status also predicts such a decline, except at the highest levels.

RELIGIOUS CULTURE

It is to be expected that there would be little support for the Italian national church in America, given the traditional hostility to this institution in the Old Country. The low levels of attendance and financial support in southern Italy, combined with a strong attitude of anti-clericalism, produced in the immigrant generation, at best, an antipathy to the Roman Catholic Church, and, at worst, outright hostility. Furthermore, the early-generation immigrants were confronted with a hierarchy composed of members of an alien ethnic group, the Irish, who did not always practice the love and kindness that they preached. Finally, religion in southern Italy was a combination of superstition and festival; in America, it was dogma, financial support, commandments and church attendance. The disjunction between the two contributed further to the continuation of the traditional lack of religiosity of Italian ethnics.

The present study contains eight questions regarding the respondent's attitudes toward his church (actual religious behavior is discussed separately in a subsequent chapter). The frequency distribution for these variables is presented in Appendix Table C.3. When compared to the percentages of respondents expressing strong support for the preservation of other aspects of the Italian culture, it is clear that the traditional negative feeling toward the church among Italian ethnics

FIGURE 4.IV

Nationality Scale by Background Variables[a]

GENERATION*

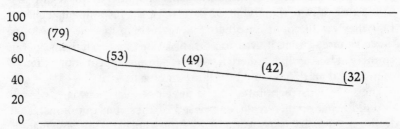

AGE*

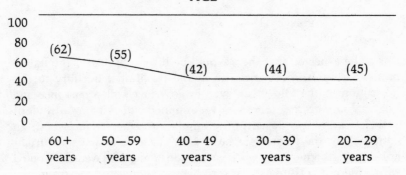

PARENTAGE*

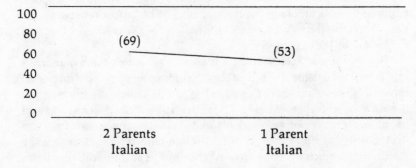

Figure 4.IV (continued)
Nationality Scale by Background Variables[a]

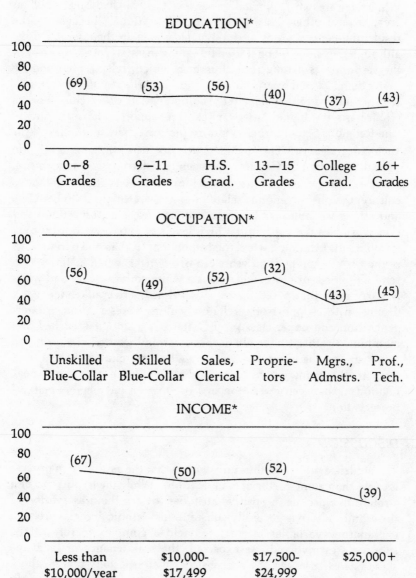

EDUCATION*

(69)	(53)	(56)	(40)	(37)	(43)
0—8 Grades	9—11 Grades	H.S. Grad.	13—15 Grades	College Grad.	16+ Grades

OCCUPATION*

(56)	(49)	(52)	(32)	(43)	(45)
Unskilled Blue-Collar	Skilled Blue-Collar	Sales, Clerical	Proprie-tors	Mgrs., Admstrs.	Prof., Tech.

INCOME*

(67)	(50)	(52)	(39)
Less than $10,000/year	$10,000-$17,499	$17,500-$24,999	$25,000+

NOTES: * significant at .05 level.

[a] The figures in parentheses are the percentages of respondents scoring high on the scale.

has not been overcome. How this attitude is related to participation in a national parish is difficult to assess with the present data set. While there are two *de jure* Italian national churches in the metropolitan area, several others may be considered "national" because of the residential concentration of Italian Americans in their service area, although they may not be staffed by Italian priests. Only 14 percent of the respondents belong to a church in which Italians predominate (more than 50% of the parishioners). Thus, while there is the opportunity to worship and to take part in the communal life of the church on an ethnic basis, few Italian Americans express support, either attitudinally (the Religious Scale) or behaviorally (national parish affiliation) for such an endeavor. The hostility toward institutionalized religion prevalent in the Old Country has been transferred to American soil.

Within the context of little support for the preservation of religious culture, the phenomenon is related in an interesting way to the class and ethnic variables, as Figure 4.V illustrates. For both ethnic and class variables there are initial high levels of support followed by a levelling off, beginning when the respondent (R) has one parent born in the USA, when he is 40 years old or younger, when he has a high school diploma or more, when he is a white-collar worker and when he earns more than $10,000 annually. While the overall tendency is a decline in the support of a religious cultural preservation in later-generation and upper-class groups, there is a stability reached and maintained rather uniformly across class and generational lines. In this instance, the effects of class and ethnicity reinforce each other, even to the point where there is slight evidence of a curvilinear relationship between generation, age, occupation and religious cultural preservation.

DISCUSSION

The evidence presented thus far suggests that the assimilation process is more than a one-factor or unilinear one. While the hypothesis of a straight-line decline in positive attitudes toward the preservation of the ethnic culture is generally substantiated, ethnic and class-related explanatory variables interact to yield a complex picture of the subprocesses involved. As expected, the maintenance of language skills has experienced the sharpest decline, especially among those persons whose parent(s) were born in this country or who have only one parent of Italian descent. Cooking skills, however, especially the number of dishes cooked, tend to persist a bit longer.

The other scales of cultural preservation exhibit distributions along the values of the background variables which indicate the interplay and counter-influences of the class and ethnic factors. The heritage and nationality scales show a linear decline ethnically and a curvilinear relationship class-wise; the destiny and religious cultural scales are somewhat curvilinear for both class and ethnicity. For all the scales, the highest degree of support for ethnic traditionalism is exhibited by the first and second generation, by those 50 years old or above and by those both of whose parents are Italian. It should be noted that except for the measures of cooking and language skills, the cultural assimilation variables are not indicators of actual behavior or even of "culture" (values, norms) itself but may more correctly be described as attitudes toward the various aspects of group culture: heritage, ethnic solidarity and religion.

The complexity of the relationships between the class and ethnic factors and the five areas of cultural behavior requires that there be further specification of the processes involved. By controlling for one or the other of the background variables, their joint effect on the assimilation subprocesses may be determined. Such an exercise is required if the curvilinear relationships observed earlier between class and several of the scales is to be properly understood. Because of the small number of cases involved when tabular controls are made and as a result of the fact that, except for the scale measuring language and cooking skills, the scales measure attitudes, not behavior, these findings are presented with the admonition that caution must be exercised in interpreting them. The figures in Table 4.3 are the percentages at each level of education for each generation scoring "high"on the several scales.[45]

By reading across the table, one can observe, for any particular value of education, ethnic behavior (percent scoring high on scale) at each generational level. By doing so, one notes the generational decline in the maintenance of cooking and language skills and in the expression of positive attitudes toward the preservation of Italian cultural forms. There is, however, less of a decline among those persons with lower levels of education. For example, compare (read across) the percentages of those with 0—8 and with 9—11 grades of schooling to those with college degrees, on the heritage, nationality and religious culture scales. Generally, at each generational stage, those with lesser amounts of education are more "ethnic" than those of

[45] In this and in the following analyses in which controls for third variables are instituted, we have selected education as our measure of class because of our belief that it is a better indicator of values, interests and life styles than broad occupational or income groupings, because it exhibits a consistent pattern of curvilinearity with a number of assimilative subprocesses and because our educational data are more complete than our occupational or income information.

FIGURE 4.V

Religious Cultural Scale
by Background Variables[a]

GENERATION*

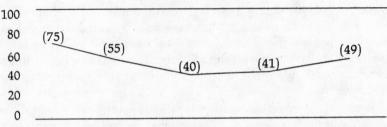

| | R born in Italy | R born in U.S., 2 pts. in Italy | R and 1 pt. born in U.S. | R and 2 pts. born in U.S. | R and 1+ grandparents born in U.S. |

AGE*

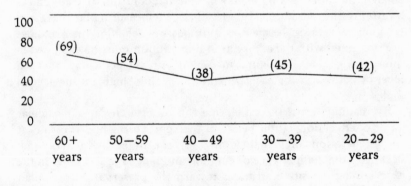

| 60+ years | 50—59 years | 40—49 years | 30—39 years | 20—29 years |

PARENTAGE*

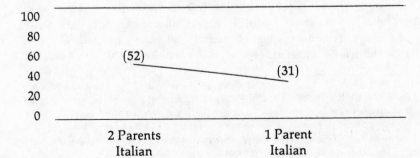

| 2 Parents Italian | 1 Parent Italian |

FIGURE 4.V (continued)

Religious Cultural Scale
by Background Variables[a]

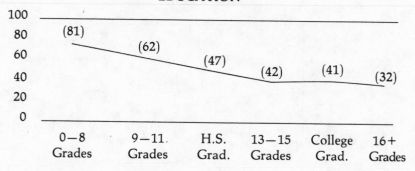

EDUCATION*

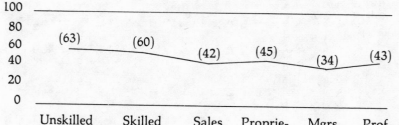

OCCUPATION*

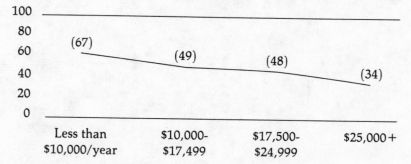

INCOME*

NOTES: * significant at .05 level.

[a] The figures in parentheses are the percentages of respondents scoring high on the scale.

TABLE 4.3

Percentage of Respondents Scoring "High" on Cultural Scales by Generation and Education*

EDUCATIONAL ATTAINMENT	GENERATION				
	R born in Italy	R born in U.S. 2 parents born in Italy	R and 1 pt. born in U.S.	R and 2 pts. born in U.S.	R and 1+ grandparents born in U.S.
Scale of Maintenance of Language and Cooking Skills					
1 0–8 Grades	50% (2)	64% (11)	—	—	—
2 9–11 Grades	100 (1)	68 (19)	50% (2)	50% (2)	—
3 H.S. Graduate	75 (4)	60 (47)	40 (20)	17 (18)	29% (7)
4 13–15 Grades	33 (3)	56 (16)	20 (5)	29 (7)	20 (5)
5 College Graduate	100 (1)	33 (9)	10 (10)	0 (9)	0 (3)
6 16+ Grades	100 (1)	88 (8)	33 (9)	14 (7)	0 (4)
					N = 230a
Destiny Scale					
1 0–8 Grades	80% (5)	87% (16)	50% (2)	50% (2)	—
2 9–11 Grades	100 (2)	87 (38)	66 (12)	80 (5)	100% (1)
3 H.S. Graduate	88 (8)	67 (63)	65 (37)	50 (36)	65 (11)
4 13–15 Grades	50 (4)	52 (29)	78 (9)	40 (10)	50 (10)
5 College Graduate	50 (2)	38 (16)	31 (13)	11 (18)	0 (6)
6 16+ Grades	67 (3)	21 (14)	54 (13)	14 (14)	50 (8)
					N = 407
Preservation of Cultural Heritage Scale					
1 0–8 Grades	100% (5)	64% (22)	50% (2)	100% (2)	—
2 9–11 Grades	67 (3)	69 (42)	58 (12)	100 (5)	0% (1)
3 H.S. Graduate	88 (8)	65 (18)	45 (42)	49 (39)	36 (11)
4 13–15 Grades	50 (4)	69 (32)	11 (9)	53 (13)	25 (12)
5 College Graduate	100 (2)	47 (17)	29 (14)	29 (21)	17 (6)
6 16+ Grades	100 (3)	57 (14)	56 (16)	36 (14)	30 (10)
					N = 399

Table 4.3 (continued)

Percentage of Respondents Scoring "High" on Cultural Scales by Generation and Education*

	GENERATION				
EDUCATIONAL ATTAINMENT	R born in Italy	R born in U.S. 2 parents born in Italy	R and 1 pt. born in U.S.	R and 2 pts. born in U.S.	R and 1+ grandparents born in U.S.
			Nationality Scale		
1 0–8 Grades	100%	56%	100%	100%	—
2 9–11 Grades	100	51	50	50	0%
3 H.S. Graduate	71	64	62	34	55
4 13–15 Grades	50	47	22	46	18
5 College Graduate	50	35	23	48	33
6 16+ Grades	100	49 *	53	36	25
					N = 418
			Religious Cultural Scale		
1 0–8 Grades	100%	71%	100%	100%	—
2 9–11 Grades	100	64	46	80	0%
3 H.S. Graduate	63	54	56	29	27
4 13–15 Grades	33	52	11	42	46
5 College Graduate	50	33	23	58	50
6 16+ Grades	100	43	20	23	45
					N = 417

Notes:

* Numbers in parentheses are base N's for the percentages. *Note:* Base N's are excluded for the "Nationality" and "Religious Cultural" scales because they closely approximate those of the "Destiny" scale.

ᵃ The base N is only 50% of the total sample because of the large number of respondents who failed to answer the questions regarding cooking habits (*See*, Table 4.1). This may be due to several factors: the question contained four sub-parts and may have caused some confusion: husbands may have thought the questions applied only to female respondents and thus did not answer them: or there may have been no Italian dishes served in the home and the respondent may have thought his non-response would indicate this.

higher educational attainment. Of particular note is the persistence of a fatalistic attitude among later generational persons with a high school education or less. This finding reflects the popular conception of ethnicity as a working class phenomenon.

Referring to Table 4.3 again, by reading down the columns, for each level of generation, one may observe ethnic behavior at each educational level. Generally, there is a decline in support for (Italian cultural preservation at higher educational levels, although the line is, in many instances, jagged. This trend is especially evident for later-generation ethnics. For example, read down the third-generation column (R born here, 2 parents born here) for each scale. All scales are consistent in their demonstration of a correlation between departure from support for Italian cultural preservation and the attainment of higher educational levels. Such an assertion, however, must be modified when referring to the cultural behavior of early-generation Italian Americans, who tended to exhibit a curvilinear, rather than a straight-line, pattern of support for the preservation of ethnic cultural forms. In the first generation especially, such support declines as education increases, until the highest level (sixteen or more grades completed), where the ethnic factor is reasserted. Thus, the high percentage of those persons in early generations with very high levels of educational attainment who express strong attitudinal support for the preservation of group culture helps to explain the curvilinear relationship between class and the cultural scales. It must also be noted that even among those ethnics at these high levels of education there is a straight-line decline in support for the maintenance of Italian culture in later generations. Since, as was noted earlier, the data indicated a "return" to ethnicity, at the middle and upper levels of class status, it must be asked whether or not these data indicate an ethnic resurgence. The concept of revival or renewed interest suggests temporal discontinuity; it implies a loss or departure, followed by a return or rediscovery. Our data clearly indicate that no such temporal break has occurred; generationally, there is an uninterrupted straight-line decline in support for the preservation of Italian culture. There is, however, a tendency for those persons who are highly educated and early-generation to adhere to the Italian language and cooking style and to express support for the carrying on of ethnic traditions, representing their propensity to be cognizant of a specifically Italian culture and to be appreciative and desirous of preserving it. Yet, even among the most highly educated levels of the Italian community "ethnicity" diminishes in later generations.

This is not to deny that there is some support for the continuation of ethnic culture among persons temporally removed from the immigrant generation. Attitudinal support, however, does not necessarily mean that those persons who express it will practice what they preach, even though American society has increasingly legitimated participation in ethnic forms of behavior. Early-generation Italians were well-suited to withstand assimilation pressures because of their spatial segregation in "Little Italies", their dependence on the family as the source of social and emotional fulfillment and their unique ability to ignore, through the practice of *campanelismo*, the influences of the surrounding society. Furthermore, there was little structural pressure, in terms of occupational milieu, to assimilate, since most Italians had relatively few skills and were in blue-collar occupations. Their lack of preoccupation with mobility precluded compromising their cultural standards to adapt to a form of behavior more acceptable from the point of view of the dominant society.

As time went on, the later generations became further removed from the immigrant culture, which became a hindrance to the realization of their social mobility aspirations. Their parents were increasingly American born, thus removing them from the parental influence of persons who had first-hand knowledge of how things were done in the homeland. They became conscious of the dominant theme of occupational mobility and financial success and of the heightened role of education and the diminished role of the family in particular and the Italian culture in general in this process. Their concern for success forced them to denigrate their own ethnic heritage because the social structural support from other mobile Italians, whose numbers were small, was limited. As Erik Amfitheatrof (1973) observed:

> The fact is that Italian Americans have always been notoriously defensive about their ethnic heritage. A proud people, they have had to struggle — like other minorities — against a debilitating sense of always having to measure themselves by Anglo-Saxon values and standards (4).

The presentation of data relating to cultural assimilation indicates that a significant degree of acculturation among Italian Americans has occurred. The research also demonstrates that the assimilation process is far from complete, as there is evidence of the persistence of ethnic values, even in later generations. The major shortcoming of most studies of ethnicity is that they are on the cultural level and thus are incapable of assessing the disjunction between the attitudinal and the social participational aspect of ethnic behavior. This study has a significant social structural component and it is the analysis of structural assimilation which is addressed in Chapter 4.

CHAPTER 5

Structural Assimilation

THERE exists considerable evidence which suggests that, in terms of occupational mobility, Italian Americans have become assimilated into American society. Harold Abramson presents data to show that they are achieving increasing representation at the middle and upper levels of the stratification system. Using 1964 National Opinion Research Center (NORC) data, he demonstrates that Italian male, white-collar employment has increased from 26 percent to 48 percent between the respondent and the parental generations.[46] A dramatic increase in the levels of education between the two generations has also occurred: 83 percent of the males in the earlier, but only 20 percent of the males in the respondent generation, had an eighth-grade education or less.[47] Greeley's analysis of University of Michigan Survey Research Center data led him to conclude that Italian Americans, with a 13 percent increase in their employment in managerial and professional categories between the 1950s and the 1960s, achieved the greatest occupational advancement of any ethnic group during this decade.[48] Under the pervasive influence of economic and political forces at the national level, the Italian American ethnic group has demonstrated its ability to meet the challenge which social mobility requires. At what cost, in terms of forsaking the traditional, ethnically enclosed social system, is the guiding question of the discussion of structural assimilation.

This chapter is concerned initially with an examination of later-generational behavior in terms of secondary associations, those which are instrumental, relatively impersonal, segmental and without strong emotional involvement. The two measures of secondary association are organizational participation and utilization of "professional" services (doctor, lawyer, dentist, clergy). The assumption here of straight-line assimilation

---

[46] Harold Abramson, *Ethnic Diversity in Catholic America*. New York: John Wiley and Sons, 1973. P. 41.

[47] *Ibid*. P. 44.

[48] Andrew M. Greeley, *Ethnicity in the United States*. New York: John Wiley and Sons, 1974. P. 77.

leads to the prediction of a declining ethnic-boundedness in these areas among later-generation Italians and those at higher occupational levels.

The second part of this section discusses the primary group relationships of Italian ethnics. Primary group relations are characterized by being face-to-face, diffuse, permanent, non-instrumental and affective. There are two types of associations which have these characteristics: the family and the friends. Our hypothesis of straight-line assimilation predicts a decline in the extensiveness and intensity of primary relationships with other Italian ethnics and, as a consequence, an increasingly larger role for non-Italians in such associations.

PATTERNS OF SECONDARY ASSOCIATION

Organizational Participation

The distrust of outsiders characteristic of the southern Italian peasant society was transported to the New World by the immigrants and transferred to American institutions: the government, employers and the church. The congregation of Italians in compact settlements served as one factor insulating them from extraneous influences. Another was the mutual aid or death benefit societies. Such institutions, whose membership was usually limited to one's kin group or to persons who came from the same village in Italy, flourished in every major city in which Italians settled in the late nineteenth and early twentieth centuries. These societies played a significant role in the lives of early-generation Italians. By providing financial benefits in time of sickness or death, they precluded the necessity of going outside the group if such services were required. What was often lost in economy and efficiency was made up for in the empathic understanding needed in times of stress. Such sympathy could be generated only by those who shared one's sense of common destiny. Furthermore, these organizations also served an important social and recreational function and, unbeknown to the memberships, helped to preserve ethnic customs a bit longer than would otherwise have been the case. The mutual aid society was more than likely the only formally organized institution in which the earlier-generation Italian Americans participated. As mobility needs dictated and his interests became less parochial, the Italian American became involved in the whole range of institutions available in the community: banks, insurance companies, churches, as well as fraternal, service and social organizations.

The measurement of the type and extent of the present organizational participation of contemporary Italian Americans indicates that 53 percent of the respondents belonged to no organization, 24 percent to one, 13 percent to two, and 10 percent to three or more. Those clubs or organizations which are recreational or social in character are by far the most popular of those joined by Italian Americans (27% of the sample belonged), followed by those established on an ethnic group basis (15% of the sample belonged). For this reason, further analysis is concerned with the predominant type of organizational activity of contemporary Italian Americans: recreational, within ethnic social clubs.

Examination of the data reveals that there is a tendency for older, earlier generation ethnics to belong to clubs which attract mainly Italians. Thirty percent of first-generation Italians and 23 percent of those 60 years of age or older belong to an Italian club. This compares to 5 percent of the fourth generation and 12 percent of those under 30 years of age who report such membership. There is evidence, however, of a slight degree of curvilinearity in the relationship between class and participation in Italian clubs and organizations: twenty percent of those with grade-school educations belong to an Italian organization; the middle levels of schooling show a decline, followed by an increase to 25 percent of those who have gone beyond four years of college. Occupation has a similar relationship with Italian organizational participation. It appears, thus, that an ethclass factor, similar to the one observed earlier in the process of cultural assimilation, is involved in the current phenomenon.   .

These data, like those presented earlier on cultural behavior, demonstrate the complexity of the assimilation process. On the one hand, earlier generations are more likely to belong to an Italian club; on the other hand, later generations, because middle class, are more likely than working class people to join organizations, although this does not explain why they join clubs with other Italians. Table 5.1 indicates that the relatively high rate of participation in Italian clubs characteristic of highly educated, early-generation Italians helps to explain the curvilinear relationship just noted. The greatest incidence of Italian organizational membership at the early levels of generation (first three columns) is attained for the more-than-sixteen-years-of-schooling category. Even among this high participational group, later-generation movement predicts a straight-line decline in the rate of membership in ethnic organizations. At later stages in the generational progression of the group, it appears that belonging to an ethnic club tends to be more of a working than a middle-class phenomenon. Thus, class, or at least education, is the crucial determinant of Italian organization participation.

TABLE 5.1

Percentage of Respondents Belonging to
Italian Organizations by Generation and Education

	GENERATION				
Education	R born in Italy	R born in U.S. 2 parents born in Italy	R and 1 pt. born in U.S.	R and 2 pts. born in U.S.	R and 1+ grandparents born in U.S.
0–8 Grades	40% (5)	18% (22)	0% (2)	0% (2)	—
9–11 Grades	33 (3)	7 (42)	0 (12)	40 (5)	0% (1)
H.S. Graduate	13 (8)	15 (78)	14 (42)	8 (39)	18 (11)
13–15 Grades	25 (4)	28 (32)	22 (9)	23 (13)	0 (12)
College Graduate	0 (2)	12 (17)	14 (14)	10 (21)	0 (6)
16+ Grades	100 (3)	36 (14)	31 (16)	7 (14)	0 (10)

N = 459

The process is one in which early-generation ethnics (first and second) join Italian clubs not only because of the insurance benefits they derive, at least from the original organizations, but also because they prefer associating with others who are of the same class and ethnicity as they. Such affiliations are a convenient source of compatible others, who share not only common educational and occupational backgrounds but also similar ethnic experiences. Later-generational movement appears to divide the ethnic groups into two broad class groupings: those in the working and lower-middle classes and those who occupy higher positions in the stratification system. For the former, the Italian club performs a function by providing a meeting ground for such ethnics, who are probably relatively unassimilated and for whom participation in social functions on an ethnic basis is an important consideration. For the latter, higher class standing heightens the concern for status and, hence, with the status-conferring capacity of organizational affiliation. The exclusively ethnic club is limited in its ability to perform this task. Furthermore, if a person is temporally distant (later-generation) from his ethnic beginnings, he is likely to feel estranged from other ethnics in the organization, for whom ethnicity is still important as a basis of communality. Later-generation, middle class Italians apparently are discovering that they can achieve a higher status and associate with others of similar interests and life styles through membership in clubs which are not organized around the ethnic factor.

PROFESSIONAL SERVICES

Generally, mass movements of people do not contain large numbers of professional persons. This is because economic betterment, the prime motivating force in most migrations, is not a factor for those at the upper levels of the stratification system. The Italian case is no exception, but the consequences for southern Italians who came to this country during the period of mass migration were especially severe, for their value system prevented them from seeking professional help, especially from foreign practitioners. Not that they utilized these services in the Old Country, but their arrival in a strange land with different customs, laws, health practices and religious precepts was the cause of much misunderstanding and hardship which could have been avoided had early arrivals legitimated contact with American professionals. Eventually, the descendents of the immigrant generation ascended to these positions, which meant that it was possible to seek help with one's health, religious and legal troubles from a person who had both the professional and ethnic qualifications to be of assistance.

The extent to which contemporary Italian Americans utilize a number of professional services within ethnic and religious boundaries was measured in this study. The overwhelming majority (98%) of the respondents indicated that the clergyman with whom they deal most frequently has the same religion and/or nationality that they do. Only 32 percent of the total report that this person has the same religion and nationality as they. This disparity reflects the effects of both availability and desirability. Availability is a factor because of the lack of Italian American priests as a result of the traditional antipathy to the Catholic Church and its dominance in America by persons of Irish extraction. This factor necessarily limits the number of Italians who can have an Italian priest, independent of the prevalence of the desire to do so. Furthermore, many, if not most, Italians have expressed an implicit apathy toward having an Italian clergyman by their relocation to neighborhoods which are non-Italian and, therefore, unlikely to be staffed by Italian clergy. In other words, they do not care about the ethnic background of their priest.

With regard to the other professionals, there are only slight variations in the patterns of utilization of ethnic doctors, lawyers and dentists. The ethno-religious factor is most crucial in selecting a lawyer, for 43 percent of the respondents reported having an attorney of the same ethnicity and religion as they, compared to 33 percent who reported having one of a different religion and ethnicity. The comparable figures for doctors and dentists is 37 percent — 37 percent — 35 percent — 42 percent, respectively. Furthermore, there is a straight-line decline, in later generations and in higher classes, in the utilization of professional services on an ethno-religious basis (See, Appendix Table C.4).

There is also a tendency toward ethnic and religious cumulativeness in the utilization of professional services. That is, those persons who have one professional of the same ethnicity and religion as they, are likely to have others of their own ethnic and religious background.

Based on the fact that it is the most highly correlated with the other three professionals in the scale, one's lawyer is the best predictor of the entire structure of professional service utilization. It also exhibits the greatest degree of decline in later generations. While 60 percent of the first generation have a lawyer whose ethnic-religious background is the same as theirs, only 25 percent of those persons with one or more grandparents born in this country do so. Thus, selection of an attorney on the basis of ethnic and religious characteristics may be a harbinger of the direction in which the ethno-religious boundedness of professional service utilization will go.

The selection of professionals is an example of the coercive, unconscious type of ethnicity characteristic of early-generation Italians. As it became legitimate for ethnics to avail themselves of such services, choices were made not necessarily on the basis of technical qualifications but rather, as Greeley likes to say, on the basis of the fact that "my mother knew your mother". For later-generation ethnics a much more conscious, rationalistic searching out process occurs. There is a greater awareness of and appreciation for selection criteria other than religion and ethnicity. The geographical movement out of the Italian enclaves facilitates the development of a more discriminating and inclusive set of standards for assessing professional qualifications. It seems that this process has progressed the furthest for the selection of legal counsel, which may be indicative of the greater availability of ethnic attorneys and/or the primacy among contemporary Italian Americans of concern for their legal, as opposed to their health or religious, affairs.

PATTERNS OF PRIMARY ASSOCIATION

The Family

The family is particularly important in studying the persistence of any behavioral or cultural pattern, since it is the societal unit which is the repository of culture and the main agent of socialization. It, thus, passes the learned ways of thinking and doing from one generation to the next and is the major mechanism by which cultural continuity is maintained. We have already seen the significant role which one's family played in the Old Country; it was the center of social interaction and of mutual aid and served as an organizing principle in the peasant villages by setting the limits to a social and areal space beyond which one tread only at his own peril. Moreover, since the peasant society was highly integrated, all institutions were tied together, with the family serving as the aegis under which they were all united. While this arrangement was certainly coercive, it generated trust and direct, intuitive sensitivity among the members it controlled. Since the Italian family is the Italian ethnic group, a dimunition of the role of the former implies the decline of the latter and is evidence of structural assimilation.

Data developed in the present study indicate the continuation of close ties among all kin members. However, there is a decline in the closeness of such relationships in later generations and among those at higher educational and occupational levels.[49] The ethnic factor (generation and parentage) predicts consistent, virtually straight-line decline in the traditional, close knit Italian family. Such a trend is highlighted in the difference which having two parents of Italian descent makes. Those with only one Italian parent feel less close to their relatives, except for cousins and in-laws, than those whose parents were both of Italian origin. The relationship between the class factor and closeness to kin is difficult to interpret. Although there is some indication of lesser attachment at higher class levels, the decline is more precipitous for extended (aunts, uncles, cousins) than for the nuclear (parents, siblings, married children) family members. While a higher class standing seems to have little effect on attachments within the nuclear family, it does tend to diminish positive attitudes toward those relatives at a greater distance, perhaps because of an emphasis on individualism among those who are rising in the class system.[50]

Another indicator of assimilation is the increasingly larger role played by friends in the social lives of Italian Americans. In response to the question: "Think of the five persons that you feel closest to. How many of them are relatives of yours, relatives of your spouse, friends of yours or your spouse?", 41 percent of the respondents indicated that three or more such persons were his or her relatives. Seven percent said that three or more were the spouse's relatives, and 29 percent said that at least three were friends. All signs for the relationships between the ethnic and class background factors and these variables are in the direction predicted by the straight-line theory of assimilation: diminished feelings of closeness to relatives and an increasing attachment to friends. Younger, more educated, later-generation ethnics are more likely to name friends rather than their own or their spouse's relatives, as preferred associates, the hypothesis of straight-line assimilation receives empirical support in this section on the family as the data indicate that later-generation, middle class Italian Americans tend to express decreasingly intense positive attitudes toward relatives, especially extended family members, and to choose their associates on the basis of factors other than the ties of kinship.

[49] The actual question is: Below is a list of relatives (mother, father, grandparents, brother(s), sister(s), married children, aunts, uncles, cousins, in-laws). Check the box which best describes how close you feel to each one or group. Possible answers: very close, pretty close, not too close, not close at all, not alive or do not have any.

[50] We were, unfortunately, unable to obtain meaningful results by controlling for generation because of the large number of missing cases, i.e., those persons who do not have brothers, sisters or married children or whose parents or grandparents may not be alive.

The Basis of Freindship

If there is an increasing tendency for Italian Americans to associate with persons on the basis of characteristics other than kinship, what are the criteria by which such persons are selected? What are the relative priorities of associating with others similar to oneself in ethnicity, religion or occupation? Table 5.2 is based on responses to questions regarding the demographic characteristics of the respondent's three closest friends. As an explication of how to interpret these data, it may be noted for example, that the first generation is characterized by high religious (96%) and ethnic (79%) friendship homogeneity and a lesser amount based on similarity of occupation (25%). Later-generational movement, on the other hand, entails a modest decline in religious, a substantial decline in ethnic, and a moderate increase in occupational homogeneity. Several observations may be made on these data:

1. Religion exhibits the highest degree of friendship homology of the three variables. This is true across all values of all background variables. Although there is evidence of some slippage with higher class, friendship ties are largely confined to others having the same religious background as oneself.

2. As one moves into later generations and to higher class levels, class (census occupational category) overtakes and surpasses ethnicity as the basis of friendship ties. To illustrate, 79 percent of those born in Italy, but only 28 percent of those who have one or more grandparents born in this country, have high friendship homogeneity, ethnically speaking. Conversely, the percentage of respondents having two or three friends with similar occupations increases from 25 percent to 42 percent. The same pattern of association holds for all the background variables, except age, indicating the surpassing in later generations and at higher class levels of the ethnic by the class factor as a basis for the selection of friends. This pattern, of course, occurs within a context of high religious cohesiveness, so the choice is one involving others of the same class and/or ethnicity, as long as they have the same religion. Note should also be taken of the "return", for the religion, census occupational, and ethnicity variables for those with more than 16 grades of school completed. Discussion of this issue is reserved for the end of the section.[51]

---

[51] These data should not be nterpreted as indicating that earlier-generation ethnics did not make friendship selections based on similarity of class. They did, but "census

An examination of the data on the relationships between the background variables and the wider friendship choices indicates several noteworthy trends consistent with those just presented.[52]

1. A uniformly high level of class homogeneity across all values of ethnic and class background variables (range is from 88% to 99%), indicating the confinement of friendship choices to persons of similar class levels;

2. A moderate straight-line decline in religious homogeneity (from 93% in the first generation to 77% in the fourth) and a sharp straight-line decline in ethnic homogeneity (from 81% in the first to 36% in the fourth generation);

3. A curvilinear relationship between education and the three types (ethnic, religious, class) of friendship homogeneity.

The data on the respondent's three closest friends and his wider circle of associates lend support to the straight-line theory of assimilation. As later-generation persons move into middle-class positions, they are increasingly likely to choose friends over relatives as preferred associates and to select them less on the basis of similar ethnicity than on the basis of common class interests and values. Furthermore, and this is significant, there is a decided non-affinity between, on the one hand, ethnic and religious and, on the other, class friendship homogeneity. Figures 5.I and 5.II illustrate the pertinent relationships.

While ethnic and religious friendship homology are highly correlated (Tau = .39* and .41*), their association with class friendship homogeneity is less so, and even negative in the case of the three closest friends. In addition, religious and class homogeneity (Tau = .05 and .26*) are not so incompatible as ethnic and class homogeneity (Tau = −.06 and .11*). While religion and ethnicity are mutually reinforcing, friendships based on them tend to be incompatible with the development of close associations based on distinctions of class. These data question Gordon's ethclass hypothesis, which predicts that people confine their

---

occupational category" is not equivalent to class. Although occupation is one determinant of the sub-culture and pattern of social relationships characteristic of a particular stratum, as an operational definition it is only an approximation of what the concept of class embraces.

[52] The actual question is: Think of the other friends you have today. How many of them are Italian? How many have the same religion as you? How many belong to the same class as you? Possible answers: more than half, about half, less than half, none. Friendship homogeneity occurs when a respondent indicates that at least half of the persons in his wider circle of associates are the same religion, class or ethnicity as he.

TABLE 5.2

Friendship Homogeneity
(Three Closest Friends) by Background Variables[a]

	Religion	Census Occupational Category	Ethnicity
GENERATION			
R born in Italy	96% (24)	25% (24)	79% (24)
R born in U.S., 2 parents born in Italy	81 (199)	32 (192)	46 (197)
R and 1 pt. born in U.S.	85 (89)	42 (89)	42 (89)
R and 2 pts., born in U.S.	75 (92)	39 (90)	41 (93)
R and 1+ grandparents born in U.S.	87 (38)	42 (38)	28 (39)
	N = 442	N = 433	N = 442
AGE			
60+ years	76% (71)	38% (69)	47% (71)
50—59	84 (114)	34 (111)	42 (113)
40—49	82 (119)	29 (116)	44 (119)
30—39	84 (91)	46 (91)	40 (92)
20—29	80 (45)	32 (47)	55 (49)
	N = 444	N = 434	N = 444
PARENTAGE			
2 parents Italian	83%* (371)	35% (362)	48%* (370)
1 parent Italian	77 (69)	39 (69)	27 (70)
	N = 440	N = 431	N = 440

TABLE 5.2 (continued)

Friendship Homogeneity

(Three Closest Friends) by Background Variables[a]

	Religion	Census Occupational Category	Ethnicity
EDUCATION			
0–8 Grades	97%* (30)	55% (29)	38% (29)
9–11 Grades	88 (56)	50 (57)	28 (56)
H.S. Graduate	83 (171)	49 (166)	34 (171)
13–15 Grades	80 (70)	39 (68)	32 (70)
College Graduate	63 (59)	37 (57)	27 (59)
16+ Grades	90 (53)	53 (53)	44 (54)
	N = 439	N = 430	N = 439
OCCUPATION			
Unskilled Blue-Collar	92% (74)	17%* (75)	61%* (74)
Skilled Blue-Collar	81 (47)	39 (46)	32 (47)
Sales, Clerical	86 (83)	18 (83)	45 (83)
Proprietors	71 (28)	21 (28)	54 (28)
Managers, Administrators	83 (53)	36 (52)	38 (52)
Professional, Technical	76 (95)	50 (94)	31 (96)
	N = 380	N = 378	N = 381

* Relationship between background characteristic and column variable is significant at .05 level.

[a] The figures in the table are the percentages of respondents whose friendship choices are homogeneous with regard to each characteristic. Homogeneity is defined as 2 or 3 friends who have the same religion, census occupational category, or ethnicity as R.

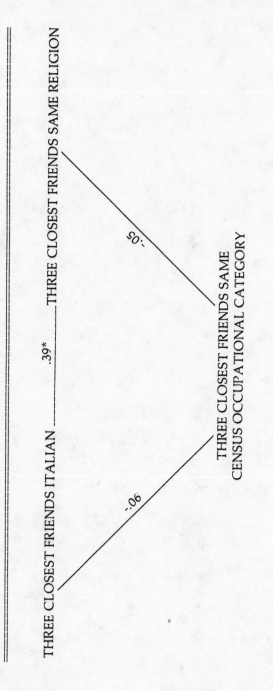

FIGURE 5.I

Tau Measurements Between Measures of
Friendship Homogeneity (Three Closest Friends)

THREE CLOSEST FRIENDS ITALIAN _____.39*_____ THREE CLOSEST FRIENDS SAME RELIGION

THREE CLOSEST FRIENDS SAME
CENSUS OCCUPATIONAL CATEGORY

-.06

-.05

* Significant at .05 level

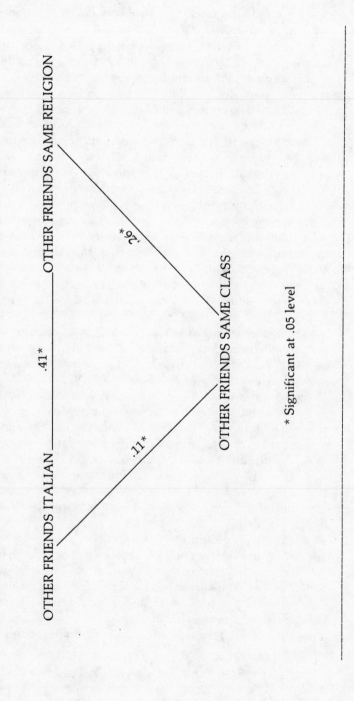

FIGURE 5.II

Tau Measurements Between Measures of
Friendship Homogeneity (Wider Friendship Group)

OTHER FRIENDS SAME RELIGION

OTHER FRIENDS ITALIAN

.41*

.26*

.11*

OTHER FRIENDS SAME CLASS

* Significant at .05 level

primary relationships to "their own social class segment within their own ethnic group".[53]

As further explication of this process, the positive association between later-generational standing and movement into higher levels of the stratification system should be recalled. As ethnics become socially and geographically mobile, they become increasingly involved in situations (neighborhoods, colleges, clubs, workplace) in which there are likely to be more persons of other ethnicities and religious denominations. In addition, the achievement of higher educational levels, a prerequisite for mobility, broadens the ethnic's horizons, gives a variety of interests and legitimates extra-ethnic and religious association. Each level of education (grade school, high school, college) draws its students from a progressively large geographic area, thereby increasing the heterogeneity of one's contacts and the opportunity for extra-ethnic and religious friendships. Furthermore, education enhances the appreciation for achievement, rather than ascriptive, standards, which may reduce the significance of those relationships based on ascribed characteristics (family, ethnicity, religion). When the middle-class Italian realizes that his varied interests cannot be appreciated or accommodated by people of similar ethnic or religious origins, he seeks fulfillment among those close at hand: work colleagues, neighbors, club members. Such persons are increasingly likely to be his class peers; religion and ethnicity, especially the latter, are diminishing in importance as criteria for the selection of friends.

The so-called "return" of those Italian Americans at the highest educational and occupational levels has been observed several times previously in this study. Specifically, such a relationship was noted with regard to the measures of cultural assimilation, Italian organizational participation and the characteristics of the respondent's three closest friends. In an attempt to explain the processes involved, Table 5.3, contains data on the degree of friendship homogeneity, at each generational and educational level, for the respondent's three closest friends. While the number of cases in each cell is necessarily small when control for a third variable is instituted, our interpretation may be justified on the basis of the consistency with which the pattern may be observed. By examining the portion of Table 5.3 which deals with the ethnic homogeneity of the R's three closest friends, a general decline in such homogeneity at higher class levels, within each generation (read down each column) may be observed. Ethnic friendship homology is higher if one has a high school diploma or less than if one

[53] Milton M. Gordon. *Assimilation in American Life.* New York: Oxford University Press. 1964. P. 52.

has gone beyond high school. Compare, for example, the percentages of those with a high school degree with the percentages of those with some college education or a college degree, across generations. Except for the highly educated (at least some college) first generation and for the very highly educated of every generation, there is a decline in ethnic friendship homogeneity. This same analysis is applicable to religious homogeneity as well. With regard to class friendship homogeneity, an increase in such homogeneity in later generations and at higher educational levels has been noted. Table 5.3 shows that such considerations are important regardless of stage in the generational process.

Based on these data and on the earlier observations of the so-called "upper-class return", a tentative explanation of this phenomenon may now be observed. Within a context of consistent, straight-line assimilation in later generations and at higher class levels, there is one group of Italian Americans which enjoys some degree of immunity from assimilative forces: the very highly educated professionals of the first and second generation. Such persons are the exception to the "rule" of straight-line assimilation. The finding that the "returnees" are the highly educated of early generations is very interesting, although calling these persons returnees is doubtful, since that term is usually reserved, since Hansen, for the third generation. They are presumably people who serve the Italian community, and, therefore, have strong incentives for never having "left". Their proclivity to express attitudinal support for the preservation of Italian customs and values is buttressed by social structural behavior: participation in Italian organizations and in ethnic friendship associations. Part of the reason for the alleged ethnic resurgence may be the attribution to all ethnics, by these persons and by outside observers, of the attitudinal and behavioral patterns characteristic of these Italian Americans, which is certainly not a group representative of the Italian American population in general.

THE NEIGHBORHOOD

For early-generation Italians the neighborhood was the spatial equivalent of the social structure.[54] Its boundaries, and those of one's social circle, were in many instances coterminous and circumscribed a geographic and social space within which one could feel secure in the knowledge that he was surrounded by other persons whom he could trust. The neighborhood provided a haven to which one could retreat to avoid contacts with strangers and to shut out the influences of the outside world which threatened to intrude on or even to destroy the

[54] Herbert Gans, *The Urban Villagers*. New York: The Free Press, 1962.

TABLE 5.3

Friendship Homogeneity
(Three Closest Friends) by Generation and Education[a]

ETHNICITY

	R born in Italy	R born in U.S. 2 parents born in Italy	R and 1 pt. born in U.S.	R and 2 pts. born in U.S.	R and 1+ grandparents born in U.S.
EDUCATION					
0–8 Grades	80% (5)	55% (20)	0% (2)	50% (2)	—
9–11 Grades	100 (3)	45 (38)	44 (9)	80 (5)	0% (1)
H.S. Graduate	63 (8)	50 (74)	48 (41)	47 (36)	45 (11)
13–15 Grades	100 (4)	50 (32)	33 (9)	31 (13)	25 (12)
College Graduate	100 (1)	29 (17)	29 (14)	24 (21)	17 (6)
16+ Grades	67 (3)	50 (14)	43 (14)	50 (14)	22 (9)

N = 438

RELIGION[b]

	R born in Italy	R born in U.S. 2 parents born in Italy	R and 1 pt. born in U.S.	R and 2 pts. born in U.S.	R and 1+ grandparents born in U.S.
0–8 Grades	100%	95%	100%	100%	—
9–11 Grades	100	87	78	100	100%
H.S. Graduate	88	81	95	69	82
13–15 Grades	100	72	78	92	83
College Graduate	100	68	50	62	100
16+ Grades	100	86	100	86	88

N = 438

TABLE 5.3 (continued)

Friendship Homogeneity

(Three Closest Friends) by Generation and Education[a]

	R born in Italy	R born in U.S. 2 parents born in Italy	R and 1 pt. born in U.S.	R and 2 pts. born in U.S.	R and 1+ grandparents born in U.S.
		CENSUS OCCUPATIONAL CATEGORY[b]			
0–8 Grades	20%	30%	100%	100%	—
9–11 Grades	33	36	11	0	0%
H.S. Graduate	13	30	42	40	27
13–15 Grades	25	26	56	25	42
College Graduate	0	19	50	40	50
16+ Grades	67	57	36	57	62
			N = 438		

NOTES:

[a] The figures in the table are the percentages of respondents whose friendship choices are homogeneous with regard to each characteristic. Homogeneity is defined as 2 or 3 friends who have the same ethnicity, religion, or census occupational category as R.

[b] Base N's are excluded because they closely approximate those in the first portion of the table.

social fabric of the community. Thus, the congregation of Italians into "Little Italies" was the result of both an attempt to preserve the "ethnic way" and a defense against out-group hostility. The neighborhood, as an insulating agent, worked well for first-generation ethnics.

As Italians moved up in the status hierarchy, they moved to neighborhoods which were indicative of their ascendancy in the stratification system. Thus, beginning at the time when the second generation came of age to take its place in the occupational world, the ethnic enclaves began to empty out. Data obtained in the present study indicate the extent to which the original Italian neighborhood has declined. Sixty-three percent of the respondents report that they have grown up in a neighborhood 50 percent or more Italian; only 16 percent live today in a neighborhood at least half Italian. Even among those of the first generation today, only 26 percent presently reside in a neighborhood where Italians are half the population or more. More generally, Kantrowitz's (1973) data, demonstrating significant ethnic residential segregation, imply the continued existence of viable ethnic communities. Several writers (Etzioni, 1959; Greer, 1961) have spoken of the ability of the group to maintain social cohesion even absent from such an ecological base. At any rate, one may raise the question of the relationship between residence in an Italian neighborhood and the continuation of particular ethnic patterns of social relationships. In posing this question, I have deliberately avoided postulating a casual sequence, for one might just as easily argue that the changes in the Italian social structure helped break up the ethnic enclaves as vice versa. The relevant query then is how much and in what areas of life have ethnic values and customs been retained by those who have migrated from the ethnic conclaves.

This study has included two variables which have a geographic basis in the neighborhood: the neighborhood itself and the adolescent friendship group.[55] Initial analysis of the relationship between growing up in an Italian neighborhood and being a member of an adolescent

---

[55] The actual questions are: How many of the people in the neighborhood in which you were raised were Italian?

Think of the friends you had when you were 17 or 18.
How many were Italian?

            _____More than half
            _____About half
            _____Less than half
            _____None

It should be noted that the neighborhood is defined by the respondent and could be one or several blocks. For a discussion of this theoretically imprecise concept, see, Keller (1968), Michelson (1970) and Suttles (1972).

friendship group composed of fellow ethnics reveals a strong positive association between the two (Tau = .45*). Also, in most instances in which neighborhood and friendship group are used as explanatory variables, the latter exhibits more significant and stronger relationships. This is because the neighborhood, composed perhaps of several thousand persons, is difficult to convene in its entirety as a group. The friendship clique acts as the intermediary between the larger structure and the individual. It is the interface of the neighborhood, which, for Italians, is usually synonymous with kin, and the individual. The friendship group transmits to its members the values of the closed Italian social system and inculcates them into its members. The message that was transferred in this manner stressed the importance of continued contact with other Italians for the preservation of the Italian way of life.

With regard to the present discussion, those persons who today are members of later-generations and who occupy middle-class positions are more likely to have been raised in a less Italian environment. Considering this decline in the ethnic-boundedness of the social context in the early, formative years, what is the effect in terms of the continuation of ethnic social relationships later in life? Those persons whose early years were spent among other ethnics in Italian neighborhoods and friendship groups are more likely to exhibit patterns of association characterized by strong attachments to kin and fellow ethnics (Appendix Table C-5). The more Italian the early environment, the more likely is one to belong to an Italian club, to have an ethnically and religiously bounded professional service network and to feel closer emotional attachment to nearly all of one's relatives. When one does go outside of the family circle to establish relationships, the ethnic composition of the neighborhood and peer group is significantly related to the characteristics of these associates. Thus, the decline of the ecologically based Italian community portends a more general dimunition of the exclusively Italian social circle.

SUMMARY

The relationships uncovered in this section on structural assimilation reveal, with few exceptions, a straight-line decline in the role of ethnicity as a frame of reference in ordering social relationships. This is true for later-generation Italians as well as for those moving into higher educational and occupational levels. While there is evidence of considerable formal recreational behavior on an ethnic group basis, such participation is characteristic of older, earlier-generation Italians, a vanishing species. The later generations have transplanted their institutions (neighborhood bars, athletic clubs, mutual aid societies) to areas of second and third settlement, where they have assumed somewhat different forms: civic and charity organizations, home gatherings, PTAs. Although some writers have been calling attention to the formation of ethnic conclaves in suburbia, we have found no evidence of such residential concentration among Italian Americans in our sample. While affluence may afford the group an opportunity to maintain its own separate social structure in its new setting, social mobility has promoted integration into the pre-existing institutional array for contemporary Italian Americans.

Perhaps the most significant finding in this section is the decline in strong attachment to kin, especially those at some distance, and ethnic friends, and their replacement by considerations of class and presumably common interests based on such similarity in the selection of close associates. While men and women necessarily differentiate themselves, the important sociological concern is a determination of the basis of such differentiation. The transition from the nuclear-family-supported-by-lateral-kin-system of Europe to an emphasis on the "nuclear" aspect of this family pattern has effected a reduction in the positive emotional bonds between kin members and has substituted extra-ethnic for ethnic considerations as criteria for social participation in primary, as well as secondary, relationships. The Italian Americans in our sample demonstrate that non-ethnic concerns, namely common class interests, values and life styles, are increasingly important in their attachment to kinfolk and selection of friends.

CHAPTER 6

Identificational Assimilation

IT has already been noted here, how the immigrant became an "ethnic" only upon his entrance into the host society. Fabian has described a process whereby "....immigrants from one society become ethnic in another". She says:

> People, while living in their own society, take their culture and identity to a great extent for granted. When, due to some historical circumstances, they leave, this unproblematical nature of reality disappears. But questions of cultural identity arise only when immigrants are asked by the host society, 'Who are you?' Significantly, the question, the context within which self-identification is requested, and the evaluation placed upon it are in terms of another culture which in some sense predetermines the answers. Hence the self-identification of the immigrant is not merely a reflection upon the old culture, it is also a response to a question posed by the host society in terms of its own categories.[56]

Thus far in the analysis evidence has been presented which generally supports the straight-line theory of assimilation. These findings would lead us to expect a declining role for ethnicity as a basis for identification among those persons who are one or two generations removed from their immigrant ancestors. Furthermore, because Italian peasants had little reason to identify with their homeland, it would be anticipated that an assigned national identity (Italian) would not endure in an alien environment.

Self-identification is formed in early family experiences through the process of "looking glass self" (Cooley, 1902), whereby one's view of oneself is shaped by the verbal and non-verbal cues of others reflecting

[56] Illona Fabian, *The Transformation of Culture and Knowledge and the Emergence of Ethnicity Among Czech Immigrants in Chicago.* Unpublished Research Proposal. Department of Anthropology, University of Chicago. 1972. P. 16, as it is quoted from Andrew M. Greeley. *Ethnicity in the United States.* New York: John Wiley and Sons, 1979. Pp. 301–302.

a person's image back to himself. Thus, the self-concept is derived from his perception of the reactions of others to his actual or contemplated behavior. The ingroup, comprising both the family and the ethnic group, is an integral part of the fashioning of self-identity. Because such ego-formation occurs early in the socialization process, the identification so implanted is likely to be durable. Furthermore, it is likely to be an ethnic self-awareness which is created, since the process occurs largely within the confines of the ethnic group. Moreover, an ethnic identity will not be a neutral one but will involve a positive evaluation, a pride in ethnic descent and an ideology, defining and legitimating "we" against "they". The creation of a self-identity would seem to satisfy a deeply rooted psychological need to feel important; one way this need is met is through a mental process of attaching oneself to and feeling part of an entity, namely the ethnic group, which extends beyond the self.

ETHNIC SELF-IDENTITY

Our measure of ethnic identity is akin to Gordon's concept of historical identification.[57] It emphasizes the social-psychological core of the shared interdependence of fate, which is based on a presumption of common ancestry.[58] Francis[59] sees this we-feeling as the very essence of the ethnic group. In our sample, 7 percent of the respondents classified themselves as "Italian", 61 percent as "Italian American" and 32 percent as American. An examination of the relationship between generation and ethnic self-identity lends support to the hypothesis of straight-line decline (Tau = .13*). Thirty percent of the first generation respondents identify themselves as "Italian" and 63 percent as "Italian American"; the comparable figures for those who have one or more grandparents born in the United States are 5 percent

[57] Milton M. Gordon, *Assimilation in American Life*. New York: Oxford University Press, 1964. P. 53.

[58] The actual question is: How do you think of yourself as an

_____Italian

_____Italian American

_____American

_____Other

It should be noted that self-identification on a mail questionnaire is not quite the same thing as identity. A more correct term may be "label"; however, the two terms are used interchangeably in the discussion.

[59] E.K. Francis. "The Nature of the Ethnic Group", *American Journal of Sociology*. 52:399. March, 1947.

and 41 percent respectively. The remainder, 7 percent of the first and 54 percent of the fourth generation, label themselves "American". Moreover, the loss of Italian identity occurs rapidly after the first generation, in which 30 percent claim "Italian" identity, compared to 5 percent of the second-generation respondents who identify themselves as "Italian". Such a finding may be contrasted with that of Goering (1971), who found an identificational return among the third-generation Irish and Italians he studied in Providence. At any rate, having both parents of Italian descent is important (Tau = .16*) for the preservation of ethnic identity. Three percent of those with one Italian parent and 8 percent with two claim "Italian" as their ethnic identification. Comparable figures for those preferring "American" as ethnic identity is 28 percent for respondents having both parents Italian and 59 percent for those having only one.

Given the high correlation between generation and age (Tau = .52*), one would expect the latter variable to be related to ethnic identity in a similar fashion, that is, decreasing Italian identity among younger persons. However, the relationship is just the opposite (Tau = −.03) from that predicted: younger persons have a greater tendency to claim Italian identification than their older ethnic fellows (Note, however, that this relationship is weak). Amongst those persons 60 years of age or older, 8 percent prefer "Italian" as their ethnic identity; among persons under 29 years of age, the comparable figure is 17 percent. Figure 6.1 contains data on the percentage of respondents within each age range who claim "Italian" or "Italian American" identity. The data seem to lend support to the ethnic resurgence hypothesis since it has already been established that younger persons tend to belong to later generations. Furthermore, if the curvilinearity of the relationship between education and ethnic self-identity depicted in Figure 6.2, is observed, it appears that there is a contradiction, because we have already "explained" this pattern by referring to the strong ethnic attitudinal and behavioral support manifested by early-generation ethnics at the highest levels of education and occupation. These apparent incongruities may be reconciled by instituting controls for third variables, as in previous tables. Again, the conclusions are tentative because of the small N's involved.

Referring to Table 6.1, we note that for each age category, there is a declining rate of "Italian" or "Italian American" identity with later-generational movement (read down each column). However, the decline is less precipitous for those in the younger age categories, especially those between 20—39. It is also instructive that no persons over 50 years of age with both parents or one or more grandparents born in this country label themselves "Italian" or "Italian American" (there are only five cases in these cells). By reading across each row, we can see that for every generation, especially the first and second (row 1 and 2), there is increasing ethnic identity among younger persons. It appears, therefore, that at least a partial explanation of the curvilinear relationship observed in Figure 6.I is that young, early-generation ethnics are labelling themselves "Italian" or "Italian American", at

FIGURE 6.I

"Italian or "Italian American"
Self-Identity by Age Group[a]

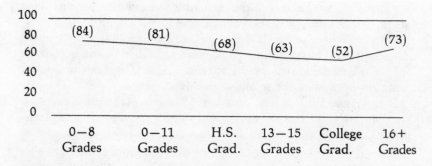

NOTE: [a] The figures in parentheses are the percentage of respondents who claim "Italian" or "Italian American" identity.

least partly because they are still close, generationally speaking, to the immigrant experience. Also, young persons in general are more willing to accept fads and trends, and ethnic identity may be a reflection of their jumping on the "bandwagon" of ethnic pride and awareness which has been legitimated in the last several years. (We will say more about this phenomenon in Chapter 12). They have also not been around long enough to have lived through a period in direct and not-so-direct assaults on their ethnic background and culture. Moreover, it is safe now; as class position is assured and society says it is alright, one can more easily be ethnic.

Table 6:2 depicts a pattern with which we are by now familiar: virtual straight-line decline in the expression of ethnicity, with a reversal of this trend at the highest educational level. Some of the younger Italian Americans are more than likely represented in this category, but their exact location, educationally speaking, cannot be determined. It may be conjectured that some of these young ethnics with strong Italian identities are recent arrivals from Italy in as much as the quota system adopted following World War II not only restricted the numbers of immigrants to be admitted but also imposed strict controls on them, favoring those with more education.

DISCUSSION

To summarize the major findings regarding ethnic identification: the labelling of oneself as Italian or Italian American drops drastically between the first and second generations. There is a similar precipitous decline when one has only one parent of Italian descent. Within a context of declining ethnic identity, there is evidence of ethnic identificational revival among young Italian Americans at the highest levels of education. Its underpinnings, at this point in the analysis, however, appear to be only cultural and intellectual, since there is no evidence of a corresponding resurgence in association on an ethnic basis.

The self-hatred which accompanied the burden of ethnicity imposed on early generations by the larger society has all but vanished as a result of the recognition and legitimation of a pluralism based on ethnicity. Consequently, it is now permitted and may even be considered "fashionable" to be an ethnic. Such a description is in sharp contrast to the situation which greeted the southern Italian who arrived in the late nineteenth and early twentieth centuries. Faced with a demand for ethnic identification, these early immigrants found it difficult to develop a national identification in a country so diverse as the United States. Furthermore, circumstances were not propitious to the formation of

TABLE 6.1

Percentage of Respondents with "Italian" or "Italian American" Self-Identity by Age and Generation

GENERATION	60+ years	50—59	AGE 40—49	30—39	20—29
R born in Italy	83% (12)	100% (8)	100% (2)	100% (3)	100% (2)
R born in U.S., two parents born in Italy	76 (59)	66 (26)	67 (45)	94 (17)	100 (3)
R and one parent born in U.S.	25 (4)	62 (26)	57 (37)	70 (20)	40 (5)
R and two parents born in U.S.	0 (1)	0 (1)	59 (27)	72 (39)	80 (25)
R and 1+ grandparents born in U.S.	0 (2)	0 (1)	44 (9)	50 (14)	54 (13)

N = 455

TABLE 6.2

Percentage of Respondents with "Italian" or
"Italian American" Self-Identity by Education and Generation

EDUCATION	GENERATION				
	R born in Italy	R born in U.S. 2 parents born in Italy	R and 1 parent born in U.S.	R and 2 parents born in U.S.	R and 1+ grandparents born in U.S.
0–8 Grades	80% (5)	86% (22)	100% (2)	50% (2)	—
9–11 Grades	100 (3)	83 (41)	67 (12)	80 (5)	100% (1)
H.S. Graduate	88 (8)	75 (77)	58 (40)	74 (39)	27 (11)
13–15 Grades	100 (4)	63 (32)	63 (8)	54 (13)	64 (11)
College Graduate	100 (2)	29 (17)	36 (14)	79 (19)	50 (6)
16+ Grades	100 (3)	75 (12)	69 (16)	54 (13)	40 (10)

N = 448

alternative identities. Since he was more than likely a blue-collar or construction worker, his occupation, not being one from which much pride and satisfaction could be derived, was not viewed as an acceptable source of identification. Likewise, religion (Catholicism), aside from being too large a category, never commanded the Italian's allegiance.

The search for an identity smaller than a national yet larger than an individual one in an incomprehensible, impersonal and threatening environment compelled the immigrant to form such an identity out of that which was familiar to him. Territory, family name and early socialization experiences were the basis of the ethnic's claim to an "Italian" identity. It was not long before American society then pulled the rug out from under the immigrant, so to speak, by demanding that he renounce his new-found ethnic identification and adopt an American one. Such a demand was difficult to meet, in as much as prejudice and discrimination inhibited the ready abandonment of ethnic and self-identity. Such events as the Mafia incident of 1890—1891 in New Orleans, the Triangle fire of 1912 in Lawrence, Massachusetts, the Sacco-Vanzetti trial of 1921 and the popular, misguided notion that Italian-ness and criminality were one and the same served to break down the traditional Italian provincialism, enhance group solidarity and hinder the assumption of American identity on a wide scale.

Such was the dilemma which confronted the second generation. Because the larger society began to define him as American, it was in his interest to go along with this new definition of the situation because not to entailed stimatization as a minority group member. Such pressures conflicted with the early learning experiences of the immigrant and he found himself in a marginal position between the two cultures.[60] The struggle for primacy in choosing an allegiance was eventually won by the "American" side, in as much as "Italian" identity was not deeply engrained, having been a product entirely of American creation and the Italian became more "American" than the Americans.[61]

Thus, Simmel's formulation of out-group rejection enhancing in-group awareness obtained only for awhile, as assimilation forces very quickly, in the second generation, diminished the only recently established "Italian" sense of peoplehood. The new, positive valuation of ethnicity and the current legitimation of ethnic diversity seem to have upgraded the status of being an ethnic and increased the attractiveness of claiming "Italian" identity.

[60] Everett V. Stonequist. *The Marginal Man.* New York: Charles Scribner's Sons. 1937.

[61] For an identification pattern continuum, *see,* Daniel Glaser. "Dynamics of Ethnic Identification". *American Sociological Review.* 23:31—40. Feb. 1968.

CHAPTER 7

Marital Assimilation

ONE key measure of the degree of assimilation of an ethnic group is the extent to which its members intermarry with members of other ethnic groups and of the host society. In an anthropological and sociological literature, the term "exogamy" refers to a rule which proscribes marriage between two members of the same group, such as caste, race or ethnic. Endogamy is defined as a rule of marriage which requires that a person marry another member of his own group. These institutionalized norms are not prevalent in the contemporary United States: the terms today refer more to a pattern of preferential mating rather than to a rigidly prescribed and enforced rule of conduct.

There are a number of functions which are served by the endogamous pattern of marriage. It helps to maintain the group's interests and social perogatives; it promotes solidarity, which is essential for successful group effort; it sustains and enhances the group's behavioral style, values and cultural forms; and finally, it helps to ensure that the marriage partners will have a rough similarity of background because of like socialization experiences. In a larger sense, endogamy tends to perpetuate both social inequalities and cultural distinctiveness.

This section examined the patterns of ethnic and religious intermarriage characteristic of contemporary Italian Americans. While significant in itself, marital assimilation is also important because it is evidence of prior social structural assimilation. That is, once the members of the immigrant group have interacted with members of the host society on a primary group basis in clubs, social cliques, and other institutions, it is inevitable that intermarriage between the two groups will occur. This assumption of the straight-line theory of assimilation leads us to predict declining rates of ethnic and religious endogamy among later-generation and middle-class Italian Americans, a tendency which is a well-established empirical fact. Bugelski (1961), examining marriage licenses in Buffalo, New York, found that in group marriages occurred among Italians at a rate of 71 percent in 1930 and 27 percent in 1960, presumably at least because of later-generational movement. Ruby Jo Reeves Kennedy (1944; 1952), studying marriage trends in New Haven, Connecticut from 1870 to 1950, established the empirical generalization that ethnic intermarriage rates increase in later generations. Ethnic endogamy decreased for Italians from 97.7 percent in 1900 to 76.7 percent in 1950. That the rate is so high in the latter year is probably a result of the large numbers of Italian Americans in the area and to the fact that most of them were second generation. Abramson (1973), using NORC data obtained in 1963—1964, indicates an increase from 29 percent to 58 percent in the rate of exogamy for Italian Americans of the earlier (first and second) to the latter (third and later) generations. Also, ethnic exogamy was found to be correlated negatively with age and positively with education.[62]

ETHNIC ENDOGAMY

As Italians have become socially and geographically mobile, escaping the direct pressures of the kin group, their increasing association with members of other ethnic groups has enhanced the possibility of intermarriage. The present sample, containing predominantly second-generation ethnics, is heavily weighted toward a strong Italian parental generation. Eighty-four percent of the respondents have two parents of Italian descent, the remainder one. By definition, 100 percent of those persons born in Italy have two Italian parents; but after the first generation there is a linear decline until the point is reached in the most recent generation (one or more grandparents born here) where only 33 percent of the respondents have two parents of Italian descent.

An analysis of the marriage endogamy patterns of the respondent's generation reveals that there is a substantial decline in the percentage of marriages which are ethnic endogamous, compared to the parental generation. A brief word of explanation is required before the data are presented. A person's ethnicity is determined by that of his parents. Therefore, whether or not an endogamous marriage has taken place depends on a comparison of the ethnicities of each partner's parents. If all four are the same, there is endogamy. If all four are not the same, there is movement toward exogamy. In the present study, ethnic endogamy is defined as both pairs of parents having the same ethnicity. If one or none of the spouse's parents have the same ethnicity as the

---

[62] *See also,* Richard D. Alba, "Social Assimilation Among American Catholic National — Origin Groups", *American Sociological Review,* 41:1030—1046. Dec., 1976, Steven Martin Cohen, "Socioeconomic Determinates of Intra-Ethnic Marriage and Friendship", *Social Forces,* 55:997—1011. June, 1977.

respondent's parents, marriage exogamy has occurred. This method of categorization is a departure from the usual practice of using only the father's nationality to classify marriages.[63] Thus, instead of a dichotomous variable (endogamy or exogamy), we have a continuum along which to measure marital assimilation. This is important because this procedure permits us to distinguish between those with pure and mixed ancestry and to make more precise formulations regarding the influence of marital assimilation in other areas.

The distribution of marriage patterns for the married respondents in the present sample is presented in Table 7.1. When compared to the figures for the parental generation, these data indicate a substantial reduction in the rate of ethnic endogamy. For the parents of the respondents, 84 percent of marriages are between two persons of Italian descent; for the respondent's generation the comparable figure

TABLE 7.1

Percentages of Ethnic Endogamous and
Exogamous Marriages for Respondent's Generation

Both pairs of Parents, same ethnicity	44%
1 Parent from each side, same ethnicity	12%
No Parents from each side, same ethnicity	44%
	N = 448

is 44 percent. Furthermore, the rate of ethnic exogamous marriage increases for younger, later-generation ethnics and for those who attain higher educational and occupational levels. Table 7.2 presents data on the relationships between the ethnic and class background variables and ethnic endogamous marriage patterns. To illustrate these trends, the following empirical propositions are presented:

— 51 percent of those respondents, both of whose parents are Italian, are married to persons both of whose parents are also Italian; only 8 percent of the respondents with one Italian parent are married to persons whose parents have the same ethnic characteristics as R's parents;

[63] Harold Abramson, *Ethnic Diversity in Catholic America.* New York: John Wiley and Sons, 1973. P. 67.

— 63 percent of first-generation respondents, but only 11 percent of those with 1 or 2 grandparents born in this country, are involved in ethnic endogamous marriages (all four parents same ethnicity);

— 61 percent of the respondents between 20 — 29 years of age are married to persons neither of whose parents have the same ethnic background as R's parents;

— there is a slight curvilinear relationship between ethnic endogamy and class, at the highest levels of education and occupation; controlling for education indicates that this pattern is due to the high rate of endogamy characteristic of the highly educated, first and second generation.

With the increase in marriages outside the ethnic group in later generations, at higher class levels and among the young, there will be fewer persons with both parents of the same ethnicity available as marriage partners for subsequent generations. Because these groups will be a higher proportion of the total ethnic community in the future, this trend is significant and some might even say ominous.

With the increase in marriages outside the ethnic group in later generations, at higher class levels and among the young, there will be fewer persons with both parents of the same ethnicity available as marriage partners for subsequent generations. Because these groups will be a higher proportion of the total ethnic community in the future, this trend is significant and some might even say ominous.

RELIGIOUS ENDOGAMY

Marriages between partners of the same religion, when compared to marriages between partners of the same ethnicity, occur more frequently in general and maintain a high rate, even at the highest class levels. Overall, seventy-nine percent of the respondents in the present sample are married to persons raised in the same religion as they. In addition, 9 percent of the respondents are partners in marriages in which the mate, raised in a religion different from his/her spouse, has converted to the faith of the other. Only 11 percent of the marriages are between persons raised in different religions and remaining so after marriage.

High levels of religious endogamy are maintained across generations and classes, with only a slight degree of slippage for later-generational and highly educated groups (Column 1, Table 7:3). The decline in marriages between persons raised in the same religion is somewhat off-set by the increasing rate of religious conversion of one partner in an interfaith marriage (Column 2). The greatest increase in religious

TABLE 7.2

Patterns of Ethnic Endogamy for
Respondent Generation by Background Characteristics[a]

	Both Pairs of Parents Same Ethnicity	1 Parent from Each Side, Same Ethnicity	0 Parents From Each Side, Same Ethnicity	Total (N)
GENERATION				
R born in Italy	63%	7%	30%	100% (27)
R born in U.S., 2 Parents born in Italy	56	5	39	100 (201)
R and 1 parent born in U.S.	48	11	41	100 (91)
R and 2 parents born in U.S.	25	14	61	100 (92)
R and 1 + grand-parents born in U.S.	11	43	46	100 (37)
PARENTAGE				
2 parents, Italian	51	6	43	100 (378)
1 parent, Italian	8	43	49	100 (67)

TABLE 7.2 (continued)

Patterns of Ethnic Endogamy for Respondent Generation by Background Characteristics[a]

	Both Pairs of Parents Same Ethnicity	1 Parent From Each Side, Same Ethnicity	0 Parents From Each Side, Same Ethnicity	Total (N)
AGE				
60+ years	67%	3%	35%	100% (75)
50–59	57	8	35	100 (114)
40–49	39	11	50	100 (121)
30–39	36	15	49	100 (92)
20–29	11	28	61	100 (46)
EDUCATION				
0–8 Grades	73	7	20	100 (30)
9–11 Grades	48	8	44	100 (62)
H.S. Graduate	48	11	41	100 (171)
13–15 Grades	37	16	47	100 (67)
College Graduate	27	12	61	100 (60)
16+ Grades	35	14	51	100 (51)

TABLE 7.2 (continued)

Patterns of Ethnic Endogamy for
Respondent Generation by Background Characteristics[a]

	Both Pairs of Parents, Same Ethnicity	1 Parent From Each Side, Same Ethnicity	0 Parents From Each Side, Same Ethnicity	Total (N)
OCCUPATION				
Unskilled Blue Collar	54%	8%	38%	100% (76)
Skilled Blue Collar	29	6	65	100 (52)
Sales, Clerical	50	16	34	100 (80)
Proprietors	37	19	44	100 (27)
Managers, Administrators	32	7	61	100 (54)
Professional, Technical	34	15	51	100 (92)

NOTE: [a] All relationships between the background characteristics and ethnic endogamy are significant at the .05 level.

TABLE 7.3

Patterns of Religious Endogamy for
Respondent Generation by Background Characteristics

	Both Partners Raised in Same Religion	Partners Raised in Different Religion, Same Religion Now	Partners Raised in Same Religion, Different Religion Now	Partners Raised in Different Religion, Different Now	Total (N)
GENERATION					
R born in Italy	85%	7%	0%	8%	100% (27)
R born in U.S., 2 parents born in Italy	81	9	1	9	100 (201)
R and 1 parent born in U.S.	79	9	0	12	100 (91)
R and 2 parents born in U.S.	75	10	2	13	100 (93)
R and 1+ grandparents born in U.S.	75	14	3	8	100 (36)
PARENTAGE*					
2 parents Italian	82	8	1	9	100 (379)
1 parent Italian	64%	15	3	18	100 (67)

TABLE 7.3 (continued)

Patterns of Religious Endogamy for
Respondent Generation by Background Characteristics

	Both Partners Raised in Same Religion	Partners Raised in Different Religion, Same Religion Now	Partners Raised in Same Religion, Different Religion Now	Partners Raised in Different Religion, Different Now	Total (N)
AGE					
60+ years	80%	11%	1%	8%	100% (76)
50–59	83	5	0	12	100 (114)
40–49	82	10	1	7	100 (121)
30–39	75	14	0	11	100 (93)
20–29	74	7	4	15	100 (46)
EDUCATION					
0–8 Grades	90	3	0	7	100 (30)
9–11 Grades	87	5	2	6	100 (62)
H.S. Graduate	78	11	1	10	100 (173)
13–15 Grades	76	10	3	11	100 (67)
College Graduate	70	12	0	18	100 (60)
16+ Grades	84	10	0	6	100 (51)

TABLE 7.3 (continued)

Patterns of Religious Endogamy for
Respondent Generation by Background Characteristics

	Both Partners Raised in Same Religion	Partners Raised in Different Religion, Same Religion Now	Partners Raised in Same Religion, Different Religion Now	Partners Raised in Different Religion, Different Now	Total (N)
OCCUPATION					
Unskilled Blue-Collar	78%	9%	0%	13%	100% (76)
Skilled Blue-Collar	75	8	2	15	100 (52)
Sales, Clerical	85	8	0	7	100 (80)
Proprietors	67	7	7	19	100 (27)
Managers, Administrators	74	13	0	13	100 (54)
Professional, Technical	79	13	0	8	100 (92)

NOTE: * Significant at .05 level.

exogamy occurs in those cases in which the respondent has only one parent of Italian descent. In this instance, 64 percent of the respondents marry a person raised in and presently practicing the same religion as he/she. This compares to 82 percent with both parents of Italian descent who are participants in this type of marriage. Thus, the ethnic endogamous marriage pattern of the parental generation is crucial, not only for the ethnic, but also for the religious, endogamy of their offspring.

MARRIAGE PATTERNS OF FUTURE GENERATIONS

Thus far, the relative strength of prescriptions for marrying within the religious and ethnic group by examining actual marriage patterns has been assessed. One indication of the rate and form which future patterns of intermarriage are likely to assume is the norms which parents instill in their children regarding suitable marriage partners. Respondents in the present study were requested to indicate the degree to which they agreed with statements pertaining to the desirability of their children marrying within their own ethnicity, class and religion.[64]

If the percentages of respondents who "strongly agree" or "agree" with each statement are summed, 3 percent of the respondents profess the belief that ethnic endogamous marriage is important for their children. The comparable figures for class and religious endogamy are 12 percent and 34 percent respectively. Based on the assumption that only those persons who have responded in this manner will actually instill these norms in their offspring, and if their children make their marital choices based on these values, it is likely that the decline in ethnic endogamy observed between the parental and the respondent generation will continue into the offspring generation. Marriage within class lines will be moderately important, but inter- and intra-ethnic and class marriages will occur within the framework of religious endogamy. Furthermore, if the pattern of friendship association observed for the respondent generation (religion most important, followed by class, then ethnicity) persists into the next generation, there will be strong structural constraints pushing in the same direction as parental prescriptions. This is so because a person's network of primary associations forms the pool from which he is likely to choose a marriage partner.

---

[64] The actual statement is: It is important to me that my children marry someone of their own _____ (Nationality, Class, Religion). Possible answers: strongly agree, agree, mildly agree, mildly disagree, disagree, strongly disagree.

These trends may be further specified through an analysis of the relationship between the background variables and parental support for ethnic, class and religious endogamy. Later-generations and those persons with only one parent of Italian descent exhibit tendencies to favor exogamy along ethnic, class and religious lines for their children. Age behaves in a similar manner: the younger a person is, the less likely he is to favor marriage within his own ethnic, class or religious group.

The class background variables are related in a somewhat different manner to the marriage endogamy norms. In the instance of marrying within one's ethnic group, the relationship is curvilinear: those at lower levels of education, occupation and income exhibit the greatest support for ethnic endogamy. There is a little decline at middle levels, followed by an increase in such support by those at the highest class levels, due primarily to the desire of highly educated first- and second-generation professionals for their offspring to marry another Italian. An examination of class and religious endogamous prescriptions for offspring reveals a reversal of this pattern. The higher the standing on the occupational and education ladders, the more likely he is to favor class and religious endogamy for his children, the opposite of the trend exhibited in the instance of ethnic endogamy. The increase in support for these values is especially dramatic at the highest levels of class.

These various relationships suggest an Italian American value system which is more supportive of class and religious distinctions than it is of those based on ethnicity. Ethnics in the sample believe that their children should marry outside their nationality, perhaps because the relative low esteem in which they believe they are held by the rest of society means that they run the risk of marrying a second-class citizen if they marry another Italian American. Thus, only 3 percent of those persons with one or two grandparents born in this country and 1 percent of those with one Italian parent favored marriage to another Italian for their children. This tendency to favor ethnic exogamy is especially evident for those ethnics at lower-class levels. Apparently, for them, their perception is that ethnic exogamy means class exogamy, which means upward social mobility. Those at higher class levels enjoy a degree of immunity from these exigencies because of their more secure class status. They can afford to marry another Italian or permit their children to do so because their ethnicity is no longer a barrier to social mobility or a threat to their social status. They have already made it and need not fear the consequences of marriage to a person whom the larger society may define as a second-class citizen.

However, such persons do become increasingly concerned about the class and religious standing of potential mates for their children. The higher the class standing of the individual, the stronger the prescription for marrying within one's own class, for to marry outside the class increases the chances for marrying down. Furthermore, the greater sharing of functions in middle- and upper-class families and the involvement of the wife in the career advancement of her socially mobile husband, for example, in business entertainment activities, dictate that husband and wife be compatible. One way to insure such compatibility is to marry someone having similar background characteristics as oneself, especially education and occupation, which make the development of common interests and, hence, sociability more likely. It appears that nationality is being perceived less and less as an indicator of similar personality and values and that class is overshadowing ethnicity as a basis for marriage partner selection.

SUMMARY

The evidence presented in this chapter indicates a significant decline in the rate of marriages in which both partners are of Italian descent. Furthermore, the generally straight-line decline in ethnic endogamy for inter-generation and middle-class ethnics and the lack of parental support for norms against ethnic exogamy portend a continuous reduction in the number of families in which both spouses can point to Italy as the birthplace of their ancestors. However, a different prediction is warranted in the case of religious endogamy, which occurs and is maintained in later-generation and middle-class ethnics at considerably higher levels than ethnic exogamy. Although there is a negative relationship between the ethnic background variables and religious endogamy, movement into higher class levels arrests the tendency toward religious exogamy in later generations. Not only is the class-religious endogamy relationship curvilinear, but higher class also brings with it stronger prescriptions for children to marry within religious lines. The data on ethnic endogamy presented in this section are consistent with the straight-line theory of assimilation. However, the evidence suggest that marital assimilation along religious lines occurs more slowly and lends support to the triple melting pot conception of assimilation.

CHAPTER 8

Behavior and Attitude
Receptional Assimilation

THERE exists considerable anecdotal evidence indicating the existence of significant amounts of prejudice and discrimination against the immigrants of most nationalities.[65] It seems "natural" that such attitudes and actions should prevail, given the fact that the migrant was more than likely a peasant, spoke a foreign language, held "strange" beliefs, practiced alien customs, had a low socioeconomic status and was a member of a minority group. In this one person, labelled an Italian (or a Pole or a Puerto Rican), there could be found the combination of all the traits which placed him, by the larger society's standards, in an inferior social position. As long as the immigrant retained these traits and exhibited the behavioral patterns associated with his minority status, he could, quite conveniently, be singled out for special treatment in the form of prejudice and discrimination.

Today, one has the impression that there is less prejudice and discrimination against all minority groups, including Italians, although there is no base line of hard data upon which to make a precise determination. There are no obvious patterns of harsh treatment of Italian Americans as have been depicted as endemic during the period of mass migration some seventy-five years ago. Civil rights legislation and court mandates may be cited as important factors in this process, although there is a problem in generalizing their efficacy too far. Such government edicts may curtail or end discrimination in certain institutional areas, such as schools, clubs, residential areas and hiring practices, where elimination of prejudice is not a prerequisite to bringing about the desired result. What happens, however, after one has gained admission to a bureaucracy? Relationships with coworkers,

[65] Luciano Iorizzo and Salvatore Mondella, *The Italian Americans*. New York: Twoyne, 1971. Pp. 55—59; Robert F. Foerster, *The Italian Emigration of Our Times*. New York: Arno Press, 1969. Pp. 401—409; and Rudolph Vecoli, *"Born Italian, Color Me Red, White and Green"*. In *The Rediscovery of Ethnicity*. New York: Harper and Row, 1973. Pp. 117—125.

as well as opportunities for advancement, may still be subject to attitudes of hostility, resentment and prejudice, which are not so readily subject to change by official decree.

Other factors, such as the legitimation of cultural pluralism, the diffusion of particular ethnic forms of behavior throughout American society and movement into the middle-class have been effective in helping to reduce anti-Italian feelings and activities considerably. Furthermore, the lessened visibility of a uniquely Italian life style has diminished the potential for prejudicial attitudes and treatment inherent in a situation in which one group differs significantly from others.

One of the images which has persisted in stereotypical form is the association between Italian descent and Mafia connections.[66] (Barzini, 1964; 252—275). Although there is not necessarily a high correlation between the two, the impression that there is, is conveyed through mass media presentations, such as newspaper articles and television crime drama. The implication drawn from seeing a Mafia chieftain arrested or from viewing gangsters with Italian names on television and in motion pictures is that all those in organized crime are Italian or, worse yet, that all Italians are in organized crime. These unwarranted inferences result in at least prejudicial attitudes and may even lead to active discrimination. Moreover, there is much misunderstanding in America with regard to the origin and meaning of the term "Mafia". Gambino (1974) has pointed out that:

> Sicilians have long used the adjective "mafia" with a small m to refer to an ideal. It is an ideal of courage, strength, agility, quickness, endurance, and intelligence.... However, the word was also used by Sicilians to refer to criminal organizations in Sicily, and Americans learned only this meaning of the word from news reports from Italy (p. 268).

Once established, these stereotypes and misconceptions are difficult to correct; the process of doing so is a long and tedious one. Perhaps the most effective way to remedy the problem is the presentation of Italian Americans in roles other than those associated with crime. Another curative is social mobility. As more and more Italian Americans achieve middle- and upper-class status, they will be a constant, visible reminder that Ialian Americans are not that different from everyone else and can perform the same range of functions that members of other ethnic and religious groups can. Furthermore, the increasing contact across ethnic and class lines, especially in marriages and friendships, will help to correct the false impressions and misunderstand-

[66] Luigi Barzini, *The Italians*. New York: Etheneum, 1964. Pp. 252—275.

ings resulting from the past social distance between Italians and the rest of society.

DISCRIMINATION

Data developed in the present study reveal that there is little discrimination perceived by respondents.[67] Eighty-six percent reported never having experienced discrimination in housing, getting a job, or being promoted. Overall, four percent reported that they were discriminated against in securing a house or an apartment, 8 percent in obtaining a job, and 9 percent in getting a promotion. The data indicate a trend of a declining incidence of discrimination among inter-generation ethnics, but an increase in such behavior reported by those at higher class levels. Since the Tau measurements are low, this interpretation is tenuous, but such a phenomenon appears to be related to a greater sensitivity to these problems by these persons and to the opportunities for discrimination afforded to those whose careers are on the rise. As an illustration of this point, those persons whose occupational settings imply involvement in large, bureaucratic structures (managers and administrators) are the most discriminated against of any of the occupational groups. They report the highest rates of discrimination for getting a job and securing housing and the third highest for receiving a promotion. In addition, 79 percent of the managers and administrators indicate having experienced no discrimination in any of these three areas, the lowest for any occupational category. These data attest to the fact that, although there is little evidence of discrimination overall, the occupational framework is an important determinant of the incidence of discrimination. As long as Italians occupied lower-level positions and "knew their place" there was no need to single them out for special treatment. Since they have begun to challenge entrenched groups for positions of wealth, power and prestige, the practice of discrimination has become an important weapon in the fight to exclude them.

Of course, the figures reported here are indicative of instances of known discrimination. There may be others of which the respondent is unaware; or there may be actions which he has not taken because of the fear of discrimination. At any rate, these measures are concerned with only a limited range of activities; there are others, such as club memberships and admission to schools, which are not examined. Finally a specific act of discrimination may have one or more basis:

[67] The actual question is: Have you experienced any discrimination in: getting a house or apartment? getting a job? getting a promotion?

ethnicity, religion, age, personality and sex. It may even be a case of a person not having the proper qualifications and thus the so called "discrimination" is not that at all but rather a legitimate form of behavior. In the absence of comparative data, the question of whether discrimination against Italian Americans is increasing or decreasing must await further, more comprehensive study. The fact that Italians are moving up may increase the opportunities for and consequently the incidence of discriminatory behavior.

This analysis suggests that Gordon's theoretical framework predicting a decline in discrimination against later-generation ethnics may be inadequate to explain the processes involved. Any consideration of behavior receptional assimilation must take into account societal, as well as group properties. Historically, the last several decades in America have witnessed a decline in discrimination against most groups, as laws, court mandates and public opinion have made this type of activity increasingly difficult to maintain. Thus, those societal constraints, distinct from any properties of the group itself, such as social participation with host society members, define one set of conditions within which assimilation occurs. Milton Gordon, who seems to have ignored the significance of such conditions, perceives the occurrence of behavior receptional assimilation as the sole result of a set of processes set in motion by structural assimilation. Once the latter assimilative subprocess has taken place, the others "naturally follow".[68]

Even if one considers only group properties, this formulation may be inadequate, at least in the case of Italian Americans. Early generations of Italians, by reason of their confinement to ethnic enclaves and working class occupations, were able to avoid situations in which they were likely targets for exclusionary behavior. It was only after they began to move up and compete with those in positions of power that they became targets for special treatment. Thus, it is necessary to expand the theoretical framework to permit an analysis along the two dimensions of societal and group properties, each hypothesized to have an independent effect on the assimilation process. Placement of each set of conditions on a continuum, ranging from low to high societal tolerance for discrimination and low to high structural conditions conducive to discriminatory behavior, such as limited social mobility or substantial social distance between groups, permits an analysis of their interrelationship and of their association with other assimilative processes.

[68] For an expansion of his earlier formulation, *see,* Milton M. Gordon, "Toward a General Theory of Racial & Ethnic Group Relations". In *Ethnicity.* Edited by Nathan Glazer and Daniel P. Moynihan. Cambridge: Harvard University Press, 1975.

PREJUDICE

The usual basis of discrimination is the prevalence of prejudicial attitudes conducive to the development and maintenance of such a behavioral pattern. There is a fairly widespread feeling among Italian Americans in the sample that there is a great deal of prejudice against them in this country.[69] More than one-fourth (26%) of the respondents in the present study report such a feeling. Although such a perception is more characteristic of older, earlier-generation persons, the decline in younger, later-generations is not that great. Twenty-five percent of the first-generation respondents and 29 percent of those 60 years of age or older believe that there is a substantial amount of prejudice against Italians today. The comparable figures for those with one or more grandparents born in this country and those 29 years of age or younger are 18 percent and 22 percent, respectively. Furthermore, later-generational movement into middle-class positions has little effect on the respondents' perception of the extent of biased attitudes. With the exception of those respondents at the highest level of educational attainment, persons at all class levels exhibit roughly equal tendencies to perceive prejudice (See, Appendix Table C.6).

SUMMARY

Since the present study has relied on a self-reporting procedure to determine the incidence of prejudicial attitudes and discriminatory behavior, the actual extent of such feelings and actions may be under- or over exaggerated to an unknown degree. The fact that they may be more or less real does not diminish their consequences for the process of assimilation of Italian ethnics. For the expression of belief in a pattern of prejudice and/or discrimination may retard the assimilative movement by providing the ethnic with a reason for resisting such forces and for seeking solace within the group.[70] In this way, an ethnic group singled out for special treatment continues to be so treated because of ingroup solidarity and, hence, high visibility as a target for discrimination, are promoted by out-group hostility.

---

[69] The actual question is: Do you think there is a great deal of prejudice against Italian Americans in this country? _____Yes _____No.

[70] Bruno Bettelheim and Morris Janowitz, *Social Changes and Prejudice*. Glencoe, Illinois: The Free Press, 1969.

CHAPTER 9

Civic Assimilation

FOR there to be conflicts of values or power in a society, there must be salient issues around which disputes arise and groups coalesce. Some writers have emphasized the visibility of ethnic social relations as the basis for political action. Dahl (1961), Wolfinger (1965), Parenti (1967) and Levy and Kramer (1972) have pointed to the persistence of ethnic voting patterns, while Glazer and Moynihan (1970) and Bell (1975) have spoken of ethnic groups as interest groups. Given a situation in the contemporary United States in which there is considerable cultural homogeneity, moderate structural pluralism and a pattern of crosscutting status positions, it is unlikely that the social fabric will be seriously rent by conflicts involving basic societal values. This is not to deny the fact that there are differences in this country which often lead to conflict and that many of them revolve around issues which are specifically ethnic- or class- or sex-related. This chapter investigates several public issues around which there is differentiation and seeks to determine whether or not there is an "ethnic" position, as district from a "class" position, on each. If an identifiable "Italian" stance on civic matters can be discerned, especially among later-generation ethnics, it might serve as an organizing principle for group conflict and would be evidence that civic assimilation has not occurred, or at least is proceeding slowly. Such a finding would be inconsistent with the assumption of straight-line assimilation.

CIVIC ISSUES

Each respondent in the present study was requested to specify the degree to which he agreed or disagreed with a series of statements regarding four issues around which there has been public debate in recent years. These questions were selected because it was assumed that a person would have formulated an opinion on each and could indicate his attitude without too much difficulty.[71] Preliminary analysis has indicated that later-generation and middle-class standing are correlated with a "liberal" stance on all four of these issues, as one would expect, based on both the "cult of gratitude"[72] and "status insecurity"[73] hypotheses, which predict politically conservative attitudes among the early generations of immigrant groups and increasing liberal tendencies as generations proceed. Because of the consistent, linear direction of the observed pattern, and for ease of interpretation, the four individual measures of civic assimilation have been combined into a simple, additive scale. Dichotomizing the responses into a high and low conservative category for each value of each background

FIGURE 9.I

Civic Scale by Background Variables[a]

GENERATION*

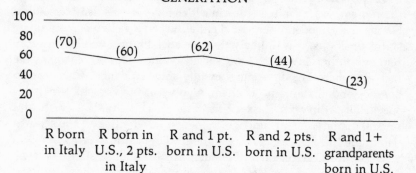

| R born in Italy | R born in U.S., 2 pts. in Italy | R and 1 pt. born in U.S. | R and 2 pts. born in U.S. | R and 1+ grandparents born in U.S. |

---

[71] The four statements are:

1. A person who is against all churches and religion should not be allowed to make a speech in this community (Freedom of Speech).

2. White people have a right to keep Negros out of their neighborhood if they want and Negroes should respect that right (Neighborhood Segregation).

3. A person suspected of armed robbery should be kept in jail without bail to prevent him from committing any crime while he is waiting for his trial (No Bail).

4. Even if a woman has the ability and interest, she should not choose a career field that will be difficult to combine with bringing up children (Woman Career).

[72] Joseph Lopreato, "Upward Social Mobility and Political Orientation", *American Sociological Review*. 32:586—592. Aug. 1967.

[73] Nathan Glazer and Daniel P. Moynihan, *Beyond the Melting Pot*. Cambridge:MIT Press. 1920.

FIGURE 9.I (continued)
Civic Scale by Background Variables[a]

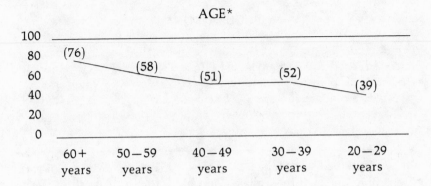

AGE*

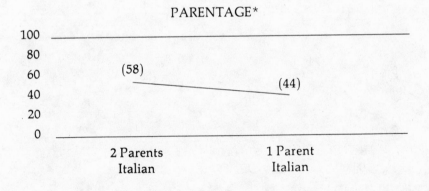

PARENTAGE*

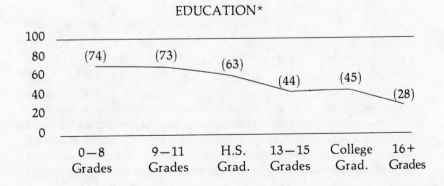

EDUCATION*

FIGURE 9.I (continued)
Civic Scale by Background Variables[a]

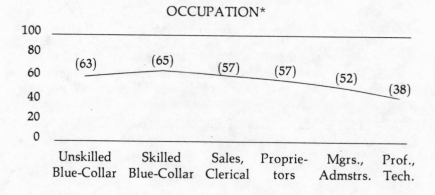

OCCUPATION*

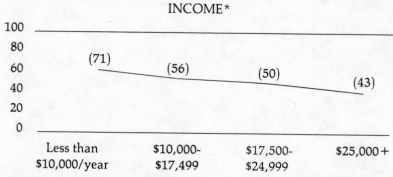

INCOME*

NOTES: * significant at .05 level.

[a] The figures in parentheses are the percentages of respondents in the "high" conservative category on the dichotomized civic scale.

variable results in the distributions presented in Figure 9.I. An examination of the shape of the curve for the ethnic (generation, parentage) and class (education, occupation, income) variables reveals a consistent pattern of straight-line decline in the degree to which respondents exhibit a "conservative" stance on these questions.

Thus, as later-generation ethnics continue to advance, socially and occupationally, they may be expected to adopt increasingly liberal attitudes on major contemporary issues. There is no evidence in the present study of an ethnic position which might retard this liberal tendency or of a third-generation or upper-class "return" to a conservative stance. Our examination of the relationship between generation and the civic scale, controlling for education, showed no significant differences in attitudes on these public issues for each category of ethclass.

ABORTION

Another area of value conflict in recent years has been that of the legalization of abortion. Chief among those involved in this debate are women's rights organizations on one side and church groups, especially those affiliated with the Roman Catholic Church, on the other. The present study listed a series of situations involving pregnancy in which abortion was presented as an alternative course of action; each respondent was asked to indicate if he or she approved of a legal abortion in each instance.[74] The data indicate surprising support for a position on an issue at variance with the moral and civic stance adopted by the Roman Catholic Church, of which the overwhelming majority of Italians are members. There is nearly universal agreement among the ethnics in this sample that abortion should be legalized in those instances in which there is a strong chance of serious defect in the baby (84%), or if the pregnancy is a result of rape (87%) or if the health of the mother is endangered (93%). Although there is less support for abortion if the woman is married and wants no more children (31%) or if she is unmarried and does not wish to marry (41%), the great majority of the respondents (77%) would sanction abortion in 3 of the 5 cases mentioned.

Within this context of substantial support for legalized abortion, what variations are to be discerned among the ethnic and class groupings in the sample? The matrix of Tau measurements in Table 9.1 illustrates these relationships. Although there is greater support for legalized abortion among later-generation and higher-class groups, this finding must be presented as an extremely tenuous one for several reasons. First, only four of the thirty-six Tau associations are significant at the .05 level. Secondly, there is variation within each set of ethnic and class variables, as well as between them. For example, while there is greater support for legalized abortion in all five instances among those

---

[74] The situations presented are as follows:
   There is a strong chance of serious defect in the baby (Defect).
   She is married and does not want any more children (Don't Want).
   The woman's own health is seriously endangered by the pregnancy (Health).
   She became pregnant as a result of rape (Rape).   .
   She is not married and does not want to marry the man (Unmarried).

TABLE 9.1

Tau Measurements between Abortion
Questions and Background Variables

	Defect	Don't Want	Health	Rape	Unmarried	Total Yes
Generation	-.01	.02	.01	-.03	-.01	-.01
Age	-.02	.00	-.01	-.05	-.03	-.02
Parentage	-.01	-.01	-.01	-.01	-.04	-.03
Education	-.06	.06	-.06*	-.03	-.01	.00
Occupation	-.03	.05	-.05	-.02	-.01	.00
Income	.05	.16*	.03	.03	.17*	.13*

NOTE: * Significant at .05 level.

TABLE 9.2

Number of Respondents Perceiving "Italian" Issues in Community by Generation and Education

EDUCATION	R born in Italy	GENERATION			
		R born in U.S. 2 parents born in Italy	R and 1 pt. born in U.S.	R and 2 pts. born in U.S.	R and 1+ grandparents born in U.S.
0–8 Grades	0	0	1	0	-
9–11 Grades	0	1	0	0	0
H.S. Graduate	0	2	1	0	0
13–15 Grades	0	2	0	2	0
College Graduate	0	2	1	0	0
16+ Grades	0	1	0	0	0

with only one parent of Italian descent, the same association is noted for only 3 instances along the generation variable. Income is the only class variable for which the signs are all in the same direction, that of increasing support among those of higher income groups. The results from this analysis are inconclusive and support neither class nor ethnic-based differentiation among Italian Americans. However, because abortion is a moral as well as a civic issue, an alternative explanation may be sought in an examination of the role of religion and Chapter 10 will consider this matter.

ITALIAN ISSUES

As indicated above, the determination of the degree of civic assimilation of Italian Americans hinges on the existence of a specific ethnic position on matters in the public sphere. Thus far in the analysis an indirect method of determining if such differentiation exists has been relied upon. Another procedure utilized involved a direct question to each respondent regarding his own assessment of the existence of specifically ethnic issues in the community. In response to the question, "Are there any problems in the community in which mainly Italians are on one side and another group on the other side"?, ninety-seven percent of the respondents answered "No". Of the 13 persons who said "Yes" to this question, eight indicated that they had done something to support the Italian side, such as helping other ethnics, voting or providing financial help to Italian clubs. With such a small number of respondents in one category, only the most tentative of conclusions is possible, but there is, nevertheless, an interesting interpretation which an analysis of the relationship between these questions and the class and ethnic background variables reveals. The following set of propositions is advanced to explain this phenomenon:

1. Persons of later generations (Tau = .01) and those with only 1 parent of Italian descent (Tau = .07) exhibit declining perceptions of Italian issues (Response of "No" to above question);
2. Persons with more education (Tau = .02) and with higher incomes (Tau = .01) exhibit a greater tendency to perceive Italian issues;
3. Persons of later generations (Tau = .04) and those with only 1 parent of Italian descent (Tau = .12*) are less likely to support the Italian side, where there is perception of a specific ethnic point of view;
4. Persons with more education (Tau = .02) and those with higher incomes (Tau = .01) are more likely to support the Italian side, where there is perception of a specific ethnic point of view; and

5. 100 percent of those persons who perceive an Italian issue in the community (N = 13) and of those who support it in some way (N = 8), have 2 parents of Italian descent.

Table 9:2 indicates the generational and class standing of those individuals who perceive specifically Italian issues in the community. Eleven of them have at least one parent born in Italy and six of these have at least some college education. The tentative conclusion drawn from these data is that the perception of specifically ethnic concerns is an ethclass phenomenon. Neither strong ethnicity nor working class status is sufficient by itself to produce an awareness of and a saliency for issues in the public sphere. Middle-class status, to perceive the issue, and a closeness to one's ethnic background (generation), for this perception to matter, are prerequisites for this phenomenon. The proper balancing of ethnicity and class result in a diversity based on ethclass and the resultant perception and possibility of value conflict. Later-generational movement into middle- and upper-class positions, however, is likely to enhance the significance of the class variable and to result in an accelerated pace of civic assimilation in this area, especially since there is little discernment of public issues having a strictly ethnic basis.

SUMMARY

Given the inherent difficulties involved in determining a dominant American value system and in accurately measuring one or another subgroup's conformity with it, this analysis has relied on the existence of a specifically ethnic position on a number of questions to assess patterns of civic assimilation. Although it does not pretend to be an exhaustive study of the whole range of issues in the public sphere, the present research endeavor has unearthed little evidence to support a differentiation of values on a strictly ethnic basis. An analysis of selected civic issues shows that ethnicity and class exhibit similar patterns of increasing liberalism in later-generations and at middle-class levels. Neither class nor ethnicity has significant explanatory power in terms of attitudes toward the legalization of abortion. Finally, there is little direct perception of ethnic problems and still less involvement in supporting the Italian side when such a perception does exist, perhaps because of the Italian apolitical tradition. These data offer substantial evidence for the proposition that a considerable amount of civic assimilation of contemporary Italian Americans has occurred and little support for the position that ethnicity serves as a focal point for the mobilization of group resources in later generations (interest group hypothesis).

CHAPTER 10

The Role of Religion

DATA presented in the previous chapter on the civic assimilation of Italian Americans indicated the existence of at least one public issue for which ethnic and class-based explanations were found wanting. This is the question of the legalization of abortion and it is our purpose in this chapter to examine the role of religion with regard to this matter and to the subprocesses of assimilation discussed in previous chapters.

THE LEGALIZATION OF ABORTION

Since nearly all Italian Americans, at least in the sample, are Catholics, a finer measure than religious denomination is necessary to determine the explanatory power of religion. In this study two measures were utilized to determine degree of religiosity: frequency of church attendance and parochial school education. It is hypothesized that greater involvement in one's faith through education and church attendance will lead to adherence to a position on abortion in conformity with that of the Catholic Church. The Tau measurements of these associations are presented in Table 10:1. Not only is the hypothesis of a negative correlation between religiosity and support for abortion substantiated in all five cases, but the magnitude of the Tau measurements and their statistical significance point to abortion as a religious, rather than a class or ethnic-based form of differentiation. However, the class or ethnic factor is not to be ignored in understanding the dynamics of this process. Although there are variations in support for legalized abortion based on class and ethnic distinctions, the effects of these variables are mediated through a third factor, which is of a religious nature. Degree of religiosity is the intervening variable affecting the amount of support for legalized abortion among Italian ethnics.

Since there is more involved than a strictly religious, class or ethnic basis for predicting behavior on this issue, consideration must be given to the relationship between the predictor variables and degree of

TABLE 10:1

Tau Measurements between Abortion
Questions and Measures of Religiosity[a]

Item	Religious Attendance	Parochial Education
Defect	-.18*	-.04
Don't Want	-.23*	-.04
Health	-11*	-.02
Rape	-.18*	-.03
Unmarried	-.25*	-.04
Total Yes	-.22*	-.03

NOTES: * significant at .05 level

    a The full statements are:

        There is a strong chance of serious defect in the baby.

        She is married and does not want any more children

        The woman's own health is seriously endangered by the pregnancy

        She became pregnant as a result of rape

        She is not married and does not want to marry the man

religiosity. The following series of propositions describes these relationships for the class background variables:

1. Class and support for legalized abortion are positively, but weakly correlated (Table 9.1);

2. Class and parochial school education are positively correlated; for education, Tau = .12*;

3. Class and religious attendance are positively related; for education, Tau = .06;

4. Parochial school education and religious attendance are correlated positively (Tau = .05); and

5. Religious attendance and parochial school education, especially the former, reduce support for legalized abortion (Table 10.1 and Table 10.2).

The following set of empirical propositions illustrates the relationships between ethnicity and the religious variable:

1. The less ethnicity (later-generation, 1 parent of Italian descent), the more support for legalized abortion (Table 9:1);
2. The less ethnicity, the more parochial school education; for generation, Tau = .18*; for parentage, Tau = .13;
3. The less ethnicity, the less religious attendance; for generation, Tau = .11*; for parentage, Tau = .10;
4. Parochial school education and religious attendance are correlated positively (Tau = .05);
5. Religious attendance and parochial school education, especially the former, reduce support for legalized abortion (Table 10.1 and Table 10.2).

TABLE 10.2

Percentage of Respondents Favoring
Legalized Abortion by Measures of Religiosity

	Support in 0—2 Cases	Support in 3—5 Cases	Total (N)	
Parochial Education				
13+ Grades	29%	71%	100%	(14)
9-12 Grades	29	71	100	(17)
1-8 Grades	23	77	100	(101)
0 Grades	22	78	100	(320)
Church Attendance				
Once a week or more	35%	65%	100%	(178)
2—3 times per month	9	91	100	(66)
Once per month	11	89	100	(19)
Few times per year	18	82	100	(147)
Never	10	90	100	(42)

Table 10.2 indicates the significant relationship between regular church attendance and amount of parochial school education, and support for legalized abortion. Those persons with a higher degree of religiosity are less inclined to express support for the legalization of

abortion. The controls for ethnicity (generation) and class (education) indicated that this relationship is constant at each level of these background variables. The inference to be drawn from these findings is that the direct effect of ethnicity and class is in the direction of increasing support for legalized abortion in later generations and at higher class levels. Each also has a distinct and different indirect effect through their association with religiosity. Those Italian ethnics who belong to later-generations and occupy middle-class positions have a greater tendency to support legalized abortion. Religiosity, especially church attendance, intervenes to attenuate this effect. If a later-generation ethnic has a middle-class status, he tends to be a regular church-goer and to be less pro-abortion than one whose church attendance is irregular. If, however, a later-generation person occupies a working class position, his church attendance is spotty and he has a tendency to express support for the legalization of abortion. Early-generational standing, at all class levels, tends to inhibit the development of support for legalized abortion.

Although religiosity is the key intervening variable, it may also be viewed as a dependent variable, the result of the mobility aspirations the parental generation have held out for their offspring. Those parents who had a strong commitment to their children's getting ahead placed emphasis on education of a specific kind: that obtained in the parochial school system. Whether as a result of this type of schooling, or of the inculcation of a set of moral values instilled in children by parents, or a combination of the two, persons who were subject to these influences hold anti-abortion attitudes. Thus, the social mobility aspirations of the parents for these children were realized through attendance at parochial schools and the two forces combined to produce individuals holding a view on abortion less at variance with that espoused by the Roman Catholic Church.

THE ASSIMILATIVE SUBPROCESSES

The data from the previous section indicate a process in which higher class status promotes religiosity, while stronger ethnicity is correlated with more frequent religious attendance and little parochial school education. Those persons having greater amounts of parochial school education are later-generation Italian Americans of middle-class status, while those with more frequent religious attendance tend to be either first-generation ethnics at all class levels or later-generation ethnics at higher class levels.

Thus, the two measures of religiosity divide the Italian Americans in the sample into two distinct groups, each with a unique set of background characteristics and assimilation profile. The data which support the characterization to be presented below are contained in Table 10:3 and Table 10:4. Those persons having significant amounts of parochial school education (later-generation, middle-classes) exhibit a pattern of substantial assimilation in virtually every area. The exceptions are ethnic self-identity and religious endogamy, where the amount of parochial school education seems to make little difference; behavior receptional assimilation, where it is correlated positively with an increase in reported cases of discrimination, and those areas having a religious base (abortion, religion of friends), where it makes a considerable difference. Those persons with more schooling in parochial schools are less likely to support legalized abortion and are more likely to have a religiosly homogeneous friendship group, especia!.y in terms of close friends, than those persons with lesser amounts of this type of education. Perhaps this phenomenon is related to the greater frequency of religious attendance characteristic of this group. At any rate, there is some evidence to suggest that those persons who exhibit this pattern of behavior are the offspring of Italian Americans who are themselves socially mobile. Those respondents with more parochial school education are less likely to have been raised in an Italian neighborhood (Tau = .07) and to have had an Italian adolescent friendship group (Tau = .08), indicating the likelihood of their parents having relocated to areas of second settlement. Lacking a strongly Italian socialization process, combined with the mobility aspirations of their parents for them, the offspring of such persons are deficient of the necessary accoutrements to prevent their departure from the ethnic traditions, customs and behavioral patterns of their forebears.

Thus, it may be conjectured that parochial school education is perceived as the means of raising one's or one's childrens' standing in the American stratification system. Concomitantly it is also apparent that the public school system is not seen as performing this function. Parochial school attendance represents the educational avenue to middle-class status.[76] If you yourself are socially mobile and desire that your progeny continue this movement, you send them to parochial schools, at least in the Bridgeport area. One of the consequences of such a behavioral pattern, whether intended or not, is that assimilation

[75] For a complete history of the relationship between early Italian immigrants and the Catholic Church in America, see, Rudolph Vecoli, "Prelates and Peasants: Italian Immigrants and the Catholic Church", *Journal of Social History,* 2:217–268, 1969.

[76] Silvano Tomasi, *Piety and Power.* Staten Island:Center for Migration Studies, 1975.

TABLE 10.3

Amount of Parochial School Education by Measures of Assimilation

| ITEM | PAROCHIAL SCHOOL EDUCATION | | | |
	9 or More Grades Completed	1–8 Grades Completed	No Grades Completed	Total N
CULTURAL[a]				
Language & Cooking Skills	12%*	30%	50%	230
Destiny Scale	45	46	62	410
Heritage Scale	45	52	56	462
Nationality Scale	50	54	54	462
Religious Cultural Scale	41	47	50	419
IDENTIFICATIONAL[b]				
Ethnic Self Identity	69%	65%	68%	451
STRUCTURAL				
Three Closest Friends:[e]				
Italian	41%	48%	44%	439
Religion	97	84	78	439
Census Occupational Category	52	39%	33	430
Wider Friendship Group[f]				
Ethnicity	58%	47%	59%	456
Religion	87	79	86	453
Class	97	95	91	448

TABLE 10.3 (continued)
Amount of Parochial School Education by Measures of Assimilation

				Total N
MARITAL				
Ethnic Endogamy[c]	28%	34%	48%	442
Religious Endogamy[d]	76	83	79	444
ATTITUDE AND BEHAVIOR RECEPTIONAL				
Prejudice[g]	16%	21%	29%	455
Discrimination[h]	10	6	4	450
CIVIC				
Civic Scale[a]	39%*	44%	61%	462
Abortion[i]	71	85	78	452

NOTES: Significant at .05 level.

a The figures are the percentages of respondents scoring high on the scale.

b The figures are the percentages of respondents who claim "Italian" or "Italian American" identity.

c The figures are the percentages of respondents who have both pairs of parents, same ethnicity.

d The figures are the percentages of respondents who were raised in the same religion as their spouse.

e The figures are the percentages of respondents who have 2 — 3 friends, same ethnicity, religion, or census occupation category as they.

f The figures are the percentages of respondents who have a wider friendship group, at least half of which is the same ethnicity, religion, or class as they.

g The figures are the percentages of respondents who feel that there is a great deal of prejudice against Italians.

h The figures are the percentages of respondents who report 2 — 3 cases of discrimination.

i The figures are the percentages of respondents who favor the legalization of abortion in 3 or more instances.

j For the sake of brevity and clarity, only the Total N's are reported.

TABLE 10.4

Frequency of Religious Attendance
by Measures of Assimilation

ITEM	RELIGIOUS ATTENDANCE		
	2−3 Times per Month or more	Fewer Than 2−3 Times Per Month	Total Nj
CULTURAL[a]			
Language & Cooking Skills	49%	37%	229
Destiny Scale	55	60	412
Heritage Scale	55	54	463
Nationality Scale	52	46	463
Religious Cultural Scale	49	51	420
STRUCTURAL			
Three Closest Friends: [b]			
Italian	49%	38%	439
Religion	87 *	76	439
Census Occupational Category	40	31	431
Wider Friendship Group: [c]			
Ethnicity	60%	51%	457
Religion	89 *	80	454
Class	91	93	449
IDENTIFICATIONAL[d]			
Ethnic Self Identity	68%	67%	452

TABLE 10:4 (continued)

Frequency of Religious Attendance by Measures of Assimilation

	2–3 Times Per Month or more	Fewer Than 2–3 Times Per Month	Total Nj
MARITAL			
Ethnic Endogamy [e]	51%*	49%	443
Religious Endogamy [f]	87 *	83	445
ATTITUDE AND BEHAVIOR RECEPTIONAL			
Prejudice [g]	23%	29%	456
Discrimination [h]	4	6	450
CIVIC			
Civic Scale [a]	55%	56%	463
Abortion [i]	67 *	85	452

NOTES :

* Significant at .0 5 level.

a The figures are the percentages of respondents scoring high on the scale.

b The figures are the percentages of respondents who have 2 — 3 friends, same ethnicity, religion or census occupational category as they.

c The figures are the percentages of respondents who have a wider friendship group, at least half of which is the same ethnicity, religion or class as they.

d The figures are the percentages of respondents who claim "Italian" or "Italian American" identity.

e The figures are the percentages of respondents who have both pairs of parents, same ethnicity.

f The figures are the percentages of respondents who are raised in the same religion as their spouse.

g The figures are the percentages of respondents who feel that there is a great deal of prejudice against Italians.

h The figures are the percentages of respondents who report 2 — 3 cases of discrimination.

i The figures are the percentages of respondents who favor the legalization of abortion in 3 or more instances.

j For the sake of brevity and clarity, only the Total N's are reported.

is accelerated in most areas, and structural differentiation based on religion is increased (attitudes on abortion, religion of friends).

Hence, persons who have forsaken the Italian neighborhood and its way of life, view the parochial educational system as the mechanism whereby their offspring will continue the social mobility process initiated by them. The commitment to this type of training reinforces the assimilation process while providing some degree of assurance that others attending such institutions will have similar religious traits and mobility aspirations. It is less likely, however, that there will be a similarity of ethnic characteristics, since attendance is usually on a territorial basis and these persons do not reside in Italian neighborhoods. This is demonstrated by the decline in ethnic friendship homogeneity experienced by those with considerable amounts of parochial school education. It is not possible with the present set of data to determine the precise motivating factor, but it should be noted that religious endogamous marriage is significantly more highly valued for offspring than is ethnic, and more so by those with nine or more years of parochial education (64%) than by those with fewer than nine (51%). Furthermore, both categories of amount of parochial schooling show an equal level of support for ethnic endogamy for their children (13%). It may be that the parental desire that children marry within Catholicism provides the motivation for the decision to send one's offspring to parochial school. According to data derived in this study, such parents may be disappointed, for there is some indication that while it has been an effective mechanism in instilling values opposed to legalized abortion (Table 10:2), it seems to have little effect on religious exogamy.

The characterization of persons with parochial school education presented above receives empirical support from several, in-depth studies of the role of religion in American life. Russo found that later-generation Italians attended church more frequently and had more parochial school education than their earlier-generation counterparts and that the latter factor was associated positively with marriage exogamy and assimilation.[77] Abramson's analysis showed that the higher the socioeconomic status of the parents, the more likely the children were to attend parochial school.[78] Attendance at a Catholic elementary school had little effect on intermarriage, but Catholic high school attendance promoted marriage outside the ethnic group.[79] High parental religiosity also encouraged exogamy.[80]

[77] Nicholas J. Russo, "Three Generations of Italians in New York City: Their Religious Acculturation", *International Migration Review*, 3:3—17. Spring, 1969.

[78] Harold Abramson, *Ethnic Diversity in Catholic America*. New York: John Wiley and Sons, 1973. P. 120.

[79] *Ibid.* P. 93.   [80] *Ibid.* P. 96—97.

Lenski's analysis of data collected in the late 1960s in the Detroit area led him to conclude that those Catholics from middle-class homes and those who are religious are more likely to send their children to Catholic schools than working-class families and those who are less religious.[81] Furthermore, those persons who have undergone this type of educational experience are more likely to be religious themselves in terms of frequency of religious attendance, doctrinal orthodoxy and adherence to views on moral issues propounded by the Church. While we have no information in our study regarding the religiosity of the parental generation, it seems safe to assume that those parents who sent their children to parochial schools were those who were more religious in their beliefs and practices.

This assumption based on Lenski's findings and on similar ones reported by Greeley and Rossi in their analysis of national data collected at the National Opinion Research Center during the winter of 1963—4.[82]

As in our study, Greeley and Rossi discovered that later-generation ethnics send their children to parochial schools more frequently than early-generation ones.[83] They also found that the higher the class standing of the parents and the more religious they were, the more likely they were to choose parochial school for their children, supporting the characterization of Catholicism as a middle-class religion.[84]

In their analysis of the effects of a Catholic school education, the researchers report several findings which conform to our own: the more parochial school education one has, the more likely he is to experience upward social mobility[85] and to attend religious services frequently.[86] Such training, however, has little influence on religious endogamy [87] (Table 10:3 in present study). Our findings differ from those of Greeley and Rossi in several respects: we found decreasing support for legalized abortion among those persons with substantial parochial schooling (Table 10:3), while Greeley and Rossi found that this factor had little influence on moral issues, although they did not ask the abortion question.[88] Our data also indicate that parochial school education is correlated positively with religious friendship homogeneity, while Greeley and Rossi found that Catholic education

[81] Gerhard Lenski, *The Religious Factor*. Garden City, New York: Anchor Books, 1963. Pp. 267—269.

[82] Andrew M. Greeley and Peter H. Rossi, *The Education of Cahtolic Americans*. Chicago: Aldine, 1966.

[83] *Ibid.* P. 82.   [84] *Ibid.* P. 41—46.

[85] *Ibid.* P. 49.   *Ibid.* P. 57.

[87] *Ibid.* P. 68—69.   [88] *Ibid.* P. 64.

had little effect on the religious characteristics of one's three closest friends in adult life.[89] The conclusion of the latter is that Catholic education reinforces the religiosity of the parents to produce offspring who are also religious; but parental religiosity has greater significance than parochial education in this process.[90]

The data from all these studies support the proposition that Catholic schools are perceived by middle-class Catholics and actually function as avenues to success. Parochial school instruction promotes Americanization in the sense of being the educational means by which middle-class status is achieved as well as a factor leading to assimilation in other areas of life. Religious education reinforces the predisposition to achieve and to be religious, which is the result of growing up in a devout, middle-class home environment.

In contrast to the characterization of individuals with parochial school education, persons with frequent church attendance are generally early-generation persons at all class levels. They are likely to have grown up in an Italian neighborhood and to be less assimilated in virtually every area (Table 10:4). The ethnic friendship group of such persons tends to be more homogeneous than that of those ethnics with less frequent religious attendance. The latter are also characterized by a greater degree of class homogeneity of friendships. This situation contrasts with that of the persons with a substantial amount of parochial school education, for whom class homogeneity is higher and ethnic homogeneity lower than for those with fewer years of parochial schooling. The closeness (early generation) and intensity (Italian neighborhood and peer group) of the ethnic experience work in tandem to inhibit erosion of ethnic values and friendships.

These findings show that Italian behavioral patterns are grounded in religious as well as in ethnic foundations. This conclusion is suggested by the positive association between religious and ethnic friendship group homogeneity and in their negative relationship to class friendship group homogeneity. Degree of religiosity, although dividing Italian Americans into two distinct groups, works in a similar manner for both by decreasing support for the legalization of abortion and by promoting the development of friendships based on religious considerations. This generalization is warranted even though those persons with substantial education in the parochial school system exhibit a pattern of considerable assimilation in virtually every other area. Thus, while later-generational, middle-class standing is associated with decreasing ethnic differentiation, the same relationship does not obtain with regard to differentiation based on relgious considerations.

[89] *Ibid.* P. 118—119.   [90] *Ibid.* P. 106.

The influence of religiosity seems to persist, even among third-generation, middle-class Italian Americans.

It should also be noted that the data do not support Herberg's thesis [91] of a religious return in the third generation. Herberg's contention was that religion, like ethnicity, is rejected in the second generation. This is so because the two are so intertwined that one must renounce his ethnicity, which entails rejecting his religion as well to prove that he is "American". The third-generation person is sufficiently removed from his beginnings that he need not dramatize his assimilation; he can thus afford to return, not to ethnicity, because the ethnic subcommunities have disappeared, but to religion, which can serve as a source of identification. Our data do not indicate a resurgence in later-generations, but rather straight-line religious behavior across generations, depending on class standing. The evidence for Italians supports Lepski's finding of increasing religiosity in later-generation ethnics.[92] One reason for this may be the absence of a close link between ethnicity and religion for this group, which means that less ethnicity entails more religiosity. Thus, the dynamics of the assimilation process, involving the interplay of ethnic, class and religious factors, may be too complex to single out one component, such as generation, and accord it equal significance for all groups.[93]

[91] Will Herberg, *Protestant, Catholic, Jew*. Garden City, New York: Doubleday and Co. 1955.

[92] Gerhard Lenski, *The Religious Factor*. Garden City, New York: Anchor Books, 1963. P. 45.

[93] *See*, Bernard Lazerwitz and Louis Rowitz, "The Three-Generation Hypothesis; *American Journal of Sociology*. 69:529—538. March, 1969; Hart M. Nelsen and H. David Allen, "Ethnicity, Americanization and Religious Attendance", *American Journal of Sociology*, 79:906-922. Jan., 1979.

PART III

CHAPTER 11

Summary and Discussion
of Empirical Findings

THE previous seven chapters have sought to determine the extent of assimilation among Italian Americans in terms of the seven assimilative subprocesses identified by Milton Gordon and have examined the relationship of these subprocesses to the ethnic, religious and class background factors of the respondents. For the purpose of incorporating the subprocesses into an integrated system, we now turn to an analysis of the associations among the subareas of assimilation. The expectation here is that assimilation in one area will be correlated positively with assimilation in other areas, based on having already established a consistent pattern of relationships between ethnicity and class and the individual measures of the subprocesses. Furthermore, it is anticipated that such a correlation will be found to be based on the theoretical prediction made by Gordon that once structural assimilation has occurred, all the others "naturally follow".

INTERCORRELATIONS OF
ASSIMILATIVE SUBPROCESSES

Since structural assimilation has been postulated as "....the keystone of the arch of assimilation...."[94] our analysis of its relationship to assimilation in other areas (Appendix Table C:7) leads to the following empirical propositions:

1. The more one tends to feel closer to his friends than to his relatives, the more assimilated one is in most other areas of ethnicity;

2. The greater the degree of ethnic friendship homogeneity, the less assimilated one is in other areas of ethnicity;

[94] Milton M. Gordon, *Assimilation in American Life*. New York: Oxford University Press, 1964. P. 81.

3. The greater the tendency to have friends of the same religion as oneself, the less assimilated one is in most areas of ethnicity;

4. The greater the tendency to have friends of the same occupational category as oneself, the more assimilated one is in other areas of ethnicity.

The data support the earlier finding of a non-affinity between ethnic and religious friendship and homogeneity, on the one hand, and class friendship homogeneity, on the other. Taken together with the relationship between the other components of social structure (neighborhood, peer group, family) and the subprocesses of assimilation established earlier, with which they are consistent, these findings point to a limited role for ethnicity in the lives of many Italian Americans today. This assertion is noteworthy in light of the fact that most researchers agree that there has been much cultural assimilation and lesser amounts of structural assimilation. The data presented in this study demonstrate that, at least for Italian Americans in the Bridgeport, Connecticut area, along with the abandonment of Old World traditions and values, there has been a substantial departure from the ethnically closed social systems characteristic of earlier generations, as well.

Based on the assumption that "birds of a feather flock together", it is probably true that all generations of ethnics have had strong, primary group attachments to others who shared common characteristics (sex, religion, class, ethnicity) and interests. As later-generation persons have moved into middle- and upper-class positions, the bases of such attachments have switched from ethnicity and class to class, largely within the religious crucible of Roman Catholicism. Thus, the locus of concern for early generations was the activities of the kinship network and of one's Italian friends and neighbors; since most Italian immigrants became members of the working class in America, class and ethnicity coincided to produce a set of common interests and a pattern of primary group behavior based on considerations of ethnicity and class; i.e. the ethclass. If an individual had a strong ethnic self-identity, favored marriage to another Italian, was desirous of preserving Italian traditions and took the conservative position on civic issues, he could expect to be supported by other Italians, who also happened to be working-class Catholics.

The movement of later-generation Italians into higher levels of the stratification system has resulted in increasing ethnic as well as class differentiation to the point where "Italian" is no longer synonymous with "working-class". This development has made it possible to sort out the influences of class and ethnicity empirically, although there is still considerable colinearity between the two. Later-generation Italian Americans occupy higher class positions than their ethnic predecessors; they also prefer attachment to friends over relatives and to associate on bases other than ethnic-related ones.

Thus, it may be predicted that a decline in the continuation of ethnic forms of behavior, for exclusively class-based primary group attachments do not provide structural support for the maintenance of specifically Italian values, customs, and identities.

This process should not be viewed as one in which the direction of influence is entirely one-way: that the decline of the role of the family leads to marital assimilation; or that association with non-Italian friends reduces Italian self-identity. Rather, the situation is one in which the assimilative subprocesses interact with and reinforce one another. While a strong, ethnic social system may enhance the individual's ethnic self-awareness, the latter also influences the choice of primary, as well as secondary, group relationships. Furthermore, the time-ordering of these variables is less important than the fact that later-generation ethnics move into middle- and upper-class positions and both these factors are highly correlated with an erosion of ethnic cultural and behavioral patterns.

There is some evidence to suggest that those later-generation Italian Americans who are not in white-collar positions or who have not attended college cling more tenaciously to their ethnicity than those who occupy higher levels in the stratification system. Table 4:3 illustrates their greater propensity to express attitudinal support for the preservation of Italian customs than higher-class persons at the same generational level. This pattern is also manifested in Table 5:3, where the data indicate that later-generation persons with a high school education or less are more likely to have Italian friends then persons who have attended college. For these individuals, ethnicity may be a source of consolation in the face of limited social mobility;[95] or it may be the other way around, that participation in ethnic forms of behavior has hindered movement into the higher levels of the status system. The time-ordering of these variables cannot be determined with data presented here, although these data do seem to suggest a continued viability for a working-class form of etnicity. Thus, class standing is crucial in determining the role of ethnicity in the lives of Italian Americans, for among ethclass groups, there was a consistent pattern of class-based, or at least education-based, differentiation within generations.

[95] Robert F. Winch, et al., "Ethnicity and Extended Familism in an Upper Middle-Class Suburb", American Sociological Review, 32:265—272. April, 1967; Michael Novak, The Rise of the Unmeltable Ethnics. New York: Macmillan, 1971.

TABLE 11.1

Percentage Change in Ethnic
Behavior Between Generations

	From First to Second Generation[a]	From First to Third Generation[b]
CULTURAL		
Cooking and Language Skills	−21%	−75%
Destiny Scale	−17	−47
Heritage Scale	−38	−51
Nationality Scale	−34	−54
Religious Cultural Scale	−33	−45
SOCIAL STRUCTURAL		
Three Closest Friends		
Same Religion as R	−15%	−19%
Same Census Occupational Category as R	+40	+60
Same Ethnicity as R	−43	−53
Wider Friendship Group		
Same Religion As R	− 5%	−20%
Same Class as R	− 5	−20
Same Ethnicity as R	−26	−49

TABLE 11.1 (continued)

Percentage Change in Ethnic
Behavior between Generations

	From First to Second Generation[a]	From First to Third Generation[b]
IDENTIFICATIONAL		
Ethnic Self-Identity	−87%	−67%
MARITAL		
Ethnic Endogamy	−16%	−67%
Religious Endogamy	− 5	−12
ATTITUDE AND BEHAVIOR		
RECEPTIONAL		
Prejudice	+24%	−36%
Discrimination	+ 5	+ 5
CIVIC		
Civic Scale	−11%	−43%
Abortion	− 5	0

NOTES:

[a] The second generation includes those persons one or both of whose parents were born in Italy.

[b] The third generation includes those persons both of whose parents were born in the United States and those persons with one or more grandparents born in the United States.

However, if it is true, as Gordon has hypothesized, that "Once structural assimilation has occurred, either simultaneously with or subsequent to acculturation, all of the other types of assimilation will naturally follow",[96] the future of Italian American ethnicity is problematic. For ethnicity is, indeed, waning as a factor in primary and secondary group relationships; this development predicts an increase in marital assimilation as more frequent interaction along class, religious and ethnic lines occurs. As a result, the ethnic group will lose its identity in the larger society and identificational assimilation will ensue. When the descendents of the original ethnic group become indistinguishable from other members of society, when the sense of peoplehood is diminished or erased because of the dimunition of the corporate identity, the group will cease to become the target of prejudice and discrimination and the locus of a distinctive set of values which might be the basis of conflicts over civic issues and, hence, of ethnic solidarity.

The inference to be drawn from an examination of the data relating to the relationship among the assimilative subprocesses is that the patterns of assimilation in each subarea are consistent with those in others. With few exceptions which are all non-significant at the .05 level, an individual who has departed from the "ethnic" way of life in one area is likely to have become assimilated in other areas as well. In general, the assumption of positive association between the assimilative subprocesses is substantiated, especially as they relate to culture, social structure, self-identity, ethnic endogamy and civic assimilation. The results are less conclusive for prejudice and discrimination, most likely because of the increasing realization of and subjection to prejudicial attitudes and discriminatory activities by those ethnics who are advancing socially and occupationally. Also, these activities are carried out by non-Italians and thus did not come under the purview of this study (See, Appendix Table C:8).

However, the ideal-typical portrait of assimilation described by Warner, Srole and Gordon receives empirical support from the results of this study. The Italian immigrant enclaves inhibited, at least initially, all forms of assimilation through their ability to circumscribe the activities of their members completely. Gradually, however, incorporation into the culture and social structure of mainstream America occurred, especially when Italian Americans became mobile and removed themselves physically and socially from the constrictions of the confining ethnic communities. Thus, extra Italian primary relation-

[96] Milton M. Gordon, *Assimilation in American Life.* New York: Oxford University Press, 1964. P. 81.

ships and cultural integration have increased, thereby diminishing the social support necessary for the maintenance of specifically Italian behavioral and value patterns.

ASSIMILATION SUBPROCESSES COMPARED

The reconnaisance of the empirical ground covered which is depicted in Table 11:1 is a crude method for determining the "rate" of assimilation in the subareas under consideration. It can be used not only to measure the departures from ethnicity within each subcategory, but also to compare the rates across the various types of assimilation, cultural vs. identificational, for example. Based on the supposition that the strongest statement of ethnicity occurs in the first generation, the table has been constructed by taking the percentage decrease in the "Italian" position from the first to the second and from the first to the third generation as a percentage of the original total. The higher the percentage decrease, the further assimilation has progressed. Before attaching too much significance to these "rates", one should recall the class composition of the various generations (Table 3:2) and that the method under discussion here does not take the class distribution of the sample into consideration.

Based on these data, the following propositions may be stated:

1. After a slow start (21% decline from first to second generation), maintenance of language and cooking skills exhibits the steepest rate of decline (75%) across generations, due primarily to a loss of Italian speaking and reading proficiency; the other forms of culture show a fairly consistent (in terms of magnitude) pattern of decline, but the degree of assimilation is not so great as for the scale of maintenance of language and cooking skills;

2. The loss of "Italian" identity occurs quickly and dramatically after the first generation; it is the most readily shed of all ethnic traits and the only one to be "rediscovered" in the third generation: a 67 percent decline from the first to the third generation in comparison to the 87 percent decrease from the first to the second generation;

3. Ethnic marital assimilation, occurring as a result of social participation in ethnically diverse primary groups, proceeds at a rate which approaches that of the maintenance of language and cooking skills scale (67% decline for the former, 75% for the latter);

4. Social structural assimilation, in terms of ethnic friendship

homogeneity, occurs at a pace comparable to the cultural and slower than identificational or ethnic marital;

5. No behavior receptional assimilation has occurred (+ 5%), but class plays a very important part in this process (*See*, Chapter 8);

6. Progressing at equivalent rates (over three generations), attitude receptional and civic assimilation occur at a slower pace than any of the other types, except those having a religious foundation; and

7. The least amount of assimilation has occurred in those areas having a religious basis; religious homogeneity of friendship group (−19% − −20%), religious endogamous marriage (−12%) and attitudes toward the legislation of abortion (0%).

Although this method is crude, it offers an initial attempt to quantify the rates of assimilation involving the subprocesses of assimilation. The application of this procedure to the Italian case yields an assimilation profile indicating that significant amounts of assimilation have taken place in virtually all areas.

CONCLUSIONS

THE data which have been presented support the major assumption of the straight-line theory of assimilation: that later-generational movement is correlated positively with departure from ethnic values and activities. It is also an indicator of upward social mobility, which is associated negatively with adherence to traditional cultural and behavioral forms. Initial analysis of the data seemed to show an ethnic resurgence among those persons in professional or technical occupations or with more than sixteen years of schooling. When the data controlled for generation, however, and relationship between class and the assimilation subprocesses were examined the "return" appears to be an artifact of the strong "ethnic" behavior of first- and second-generation persons in these occupational and educational categories. Thus, there was no third-generation of even upper-class return; the exceptions to the rule of linear decline could be at least partially explained by reference to the closeness to the immigration experience of early-generation, highly educated professionals. Their cultural and behavioral style was not a return but represented a continuation of and participation in a culture and pattern of social relationships which was satisfying to them. Even among persons at the uppermost levels of class, ethnic behavior and attitudes declined in later generations.

Moreover, there has been no indication that the function of ethnicity in later generations is to serve as an organizing principle for the furtherance of group interests, in as much as there is little perception of, let alone participation in, specific ethnic issues in the community. However, there is evidence, in the form of degree of religiosity, to suggest that religion may be such a force, especially with regard to the question of legalized abortion.

This last proposition must be viewed in conjunction with the tendency of all generational and class groupings to marry within the religious faith of which one is a member. The influence of religion in shaping attitudes on certain issues and in serving as the major criterion for marriage partner selection lends credence to the triple-melting pot theory of assimilation. Within a context of significantly declining rates of ethnic endogamy, religious endogamous patterns continue at very high levels in all generations and class levels. It has been demonstrated that the early-generation experience is an ethclass phenomenon; but as later-generational movement occurs there is a tendency for class to assume primacy as the basis of value adherence and of primary and secondary group associations and hence of societal differentiation. It must be emphasized, however, that such a process takes place within the crucible of Roman Catholicism for Italian Americans.

By making these assertions there is no intention to deny that there are residual ethnic attitudes and behavioral styles in later generations. Some third-generation Italian Americans (indeed most Americans) do not trust politicians, are inclined to be fatalistic, identify as *"Italian Americans"* and support the preservation of their customs and traditions. It does appear, however, that later-generation Italian American ethnicity is assuming several distinct forms, discussed in the final chapter.

CHAPTER 12

A THEORETICAL OVERVIEW

THE history of the development of viewpoints on assimilation is one of a progressive clarification of processes wherein the polemical tone of the earlier "theories" is increasingly replaced by an approach based on more rigorous adherence to scientific principles and methods. The increase in attention to behavior rather than attitudes has resulted in a greater understanding of the subprocesses of assimilation, but such an understanding, even to this day, has remained on the intuitive level, for there have been few empirical studies to support the suppositions of the various theoretical models. However, it is certainly true that each has made some contribution to the ongoing attempt to discern the operation of the American assimilative experience.

The three earliest perspectives are a direct product of their historical surroundings and represent themes or statements which describe how immigrant groups should behave in their host society. Anglo conformity demanded that new arrivals renounce their ethnicity and adopt pre-existing, supposedly superior "American" ways. The melting pot perspective was a bit more sympathetic to the ethnic's culture and social structure but still prescribed the abandonment of foreign habits and the adoption of a new, indigenous type of American value and behavioral matrix. The cultural pluralism ideology, which spoke of the maintenance of the communal life, identity and values of the immigrant group, gave public recognition to a reality that already obtained, namely, that American society was a mosaic of subcultures and subgroups.

One of Warner and Srole's major contributions was to introduce "class" to the study of ethnicity.[97] Gordon further specified the assimilation process with his ethclass concept;[98] persons in the same

---

[97] W. Lloyd Warner, and Leo Srole. *The Serial Systems of American Ethnic Groups.* New Haven: Yale University Press. 1945.

[98] Milton M. Gordon, *Assimilation in American Life.* New York: Oxford University Press, 1964.

class have the same values, regardless of ethnicity. Conversely, persons who have different class standings subscribe to different sets of values, regardless of ethnicity. Thus, the ethclass is the largest reference group with which Americans have a positive sense of identification. Glazer and Moynihan [99] see considerable diversity because the ethnic culture of later generations can serve as the basis for the formation of political and social groups and for the assertion of demands based on differences in ethnic values. Andrew Greeley's [100] ethnogenesis model assumes a pluralistic society composed of ethnic groups having distinct cultural profiles, or natural histories. The culture of each group has two parts: one which it shares with the rest of society and the other which is unique. The trend is for the common culture to become larger under the levelling influences of the mass media, generational movement and the educational system, producing greater similarity among groups and leading ultimately to the so-called "mass society".

The failure to perceive the distinction between micro- and macro-levels of analysis has led to confusion in understanding ethnicity and assimilation. At the macro-level, the emphasis is on society as a whole and on the degree of diversity characterizing it, whereas on the micro-level, the importance of assimilation as a process, involving change and adjustment over time, is underscored. On the macro-level, conditions outside of the group — the existing stratification system and the position of the group within it, residential patterns, how the larger society views the group — are of paramount importance in shaping the group's assimilation experience. [101] However, on the micro level, those factors internal to the group — amount of ethnic pride, level of educational and occupational skills, extent of in-group social relationships — are accentuated. An understanding of all aspects of assimilation requires, as a first step, the recognition that at least these two levels of analysis exist and that their protocols must be made explicit if empirical and theoretical precision is to be achieved. Secondly, there must be a synthesis of the two approaches into one, such as Gordon's [102] which views ethnicity and assimilation as constantly

---

[99] Nathal Glazer and Daniel P. Moynihan, *Beyond the Melting Pot*. Cambridge: MIT Press, 1970; Nathan Glazer and Daniel P. Moynihan, "Why Ethnicity" *Commentary*, 58:33-39. Oct. 1974.

[100] Andrew M. Greeley, *Ethnicity in the United States*. New York: John Wiley and Sons, 1974.

[101] *See*, William L. Yancey, *etal.*, "Emergent Ethnicity: A Review and Reformulation", *American Sociological Review*, 41:391–403. June, 1976.

[102] Milton M. Gordon, "Toward a General Theory of Racial and Ethnic Group Relations". In *Ethnicity*. Edited by Nathan Glazer and Daniel P. Moynihan. Cambridge: Harvard University Press, 1975.

unfolding, multi-dimensional processes, the result of dynamic inter-action between structural conditions and ethnic group characteristics. Thus, ethnicity and assimilation are not either/or phenomena but run along a continuum from low to high, assuming diverse forms in different historical periods, as manifested in patterns of identification, life styles, power relationships, etc. So, as Newman[103] points out, assimilation (micro-level) and pluralism (macro-level) can co-exist. While society is composed of diverse groups tending toward homo-geneity in some respects, the character of each group is being transformed in such a way that each is, in some ways, becoming different from others and from the society as a whole.

A HISTORICAL OVERVIEW

AT its inception, this country's population was relatively homogeneous (compared to what it would become) with respect to its religious, ethnic and class composition. The immigration of peoples with cultures, religions and sentiments substantially different from those of the first settlers insured that this situation would not continue for long. The advent of the "new immigration" presented the host society with a task beyond its integrative capacity and the cultural pluralism ideology arose to explain why certain groups could not and should not be assimilated. Once it became apparent that complete absorption was unattainable, pluralism was considered legitimate, for the divergence of the emergent communities and their cultures from the dominant pattern enhanced the possibility of conflict with other groups and served as a constant reminder of the pluralistic nature of American society.

Even with the progressive expansion of the common element of each group's culture, the maintenance of separate subgroups, based on distinctions of class, religion, ethnicity and their combinations, has provided the requisite structural supports for a least a modicum of value differentiation. Although there has historically been and continues to be widespread societal acceptance of certain values — respect for private property, the Judeo-Christian ethic, patriotism — there are considerable differences in attitudes and life styles at lower levels. It is unfortunate that the term cultural pluralism has come to refer to a phenomenon which more accurately could be described as structural or religious pluralism. For while all forms of pluralism have been extant, the cultural type has probably been the least developed, as

[103] William M. Newman, *American Pluralism: A Study of Minority Groups and Social Theory*. New York: Harper Row, 1973. P. 182.

immigrants have been willing to shed their cultural baggage but less amenable to deserting their ethnically enclosed kin and friendship networks. The latter has continued to serve, at least into the second generation, as the "proper" substructure for choosing close associates and marriage partners.

WORKING CLASS ETHNICITY

Generally, there are two distinct styles, or patterns of ethnicity today. The first is characteristic of the working class; it exists on the behavioral level, because ethnics live it. Predominantly middle-aged, second-generation ethnics, they practice their ethnicity — celebration of feasts and ceremonial occasions, socializing, organizational participation — within the boundaries of family and ethnic peer group. They live close enough to the homeland, in a socio-cultural sense, for their ethnicity to take on a strong, emotional tone. Moreover, their early learning experiences in the neighborhood and friendship groups insure the continuation, at least for awhile, of their traditional values and behavioral patterns. Their limited social and geographic mobility inhibits the development of pressures for change which might otherwise occur.

Working class ethnics are the visible ethnics today. They tend to congregate in their traditional central city neighborhoods where their still somewhat distinctive life styles and institutions provide evidence to the rest of society that ethnicity is not dead. Their residential clustering means the possibility of conflict over turf and jobs with other, more recent arrivals in the city, mainly blacks and Hispanics. Of late, such ethnics have become targets of community organizers, who, unlike their predecessors 50–75 years ago, see the value of ethnicity as a constructive element in a program of neighborhood revitalization.[104]

Although there has been a departure from ethnic origins, there has not been a corresponding movement away from class origins.[105] Working class beginnings, more so than ethnic, are still an important determinant of interests, politics and life styles. It is a mistake to attribute their concerns solely to ethnicity, in as much as many of them are related to status other than that of being an ethnic: taxpayer, parent, neighborhood resident. In fact, their problems transcend ethnicity and are common to the working class of all ethnic groups.

[104] Geno M. Baroni, "Ethjnicity and Public Policy". In *Pieces of a Dream*. Edited by Michael Wenk *etal*. Staten Island: Center for Migration Studies, 1972.
[105] Irving M. Levine and Judith Herman, "The Life of White Ethnics: Toward More Effective Working-Class Strategies", *Dissent*, 19:286–294. Winter, 1972.

One issue is occupation: the decline of working class status in a white-collar, service-oriented society; the fear of being replaced through automation; the feeling of dismay, as rising inflation and increasing taxes threaten to erode whatever financial gains have been made in recent years. There is the problem of residence: of living in an older, run-down neighborhood and of being unable to afford to move out; of being faced with increased property taxes; of seeing the "ghetto" move ever closer; of being made scape-goats for the problems of minorities and of being labelled "racist" when they resist government-initiated integration efforts. There is the problem of culture: the realization that working-class culture does not work in a middle-class society and that, for example, to get ahead, children must attend college, which is perceived as a threat to the integrity of the family. Moreover, these problems and fears are exacerbated because of an apolitical tradition and the rejection of formal organizations as mechanisms of change. In times of stress and uncertainty, there is a tendency to adhere to the tried-and-true formula, which is in this case, ethnicity: family, friends, institutions. For these people, ethnicity is a solace because they have not achieved the American dream.

The distinction between this kind of ethnicity and the one to be described below is crucial, for much of the basis for the claim that ethnicity is alive and well lies in the working class form. Often, conclusions based on perceptions of processes occurring in ethnic enclaves or in cities are generalized to all ethnics. Glazer and Moynihan, [106] for example, contend that ethnic groups became interest groups in later generations and support such a proposition by citing evidence obtained in their study of New York City. New York City, however, is neither Bridgeport nor the nation and has several characteristics which make it unsuitable for studying processes of assimilation relative to later-generational behavior. Historically, it has served as the area of first settlement for diverse immigrant groups whose memberships have included many working-class ethnics. Arriving serially and carving out their own piece of urban turf, these groups have often found themselves in competition with each other for scarce space, power and jobs. This contention is an oft-repeated phenomenon; hence, the emergence of the view of ethnicity as an organizing principle and of ethnic groups as interest groups. A hint that Glazer and Moynihan are talking about the working class form of ethnicity is given by their statement from the same text noting:

...ethnic identities have taken over some of the task in self-definition

[106] Nathan Glazer and Daniel P. Moynihan, *Beyond the Melting Pot.* Cambridge: MIT Press, 1970.

and in definition by others that occupational identities, particularly working-class occupational identities, have generally played (xxxiv).

A similar orientation may also be attributed to present-day practitioners in the field of community organization, whose professional interest in attempting to preserve ethnic neighborhoods may lead them to perceive a greater amount of ethnic vitality than may in fact exist. In the effort to achieve neighborhood revitalization, organizing around a vision or dream may be one element of a successful strategy. Ethnicity, in the form of "what the community was like thirty years ago", can provide the necessary imagery. At any rate, these selective perceptions and overgeneralizations give the impression of the continued viability of behavioral-level ethnicity. Furthermore, since the concern is with a predominantly working-class form of ethnicity, there is a neglect of that kind of characteristic of the middle-class, which promises to become more prevalent, since later-generational ethnics are increasingly middle-class.

THE "NEW ETHNICITY"

THE new form of ethnicity coming to be practiced exists primarily, although not exclusively, on the non-behavioral level. Ethnics of today who, as little as fifteen or twenty years ago would have downplayed or denied their ethnic origins, are proud that their parents or grandparents were born in the Old Country and boast that they have visited the birthplace of their ancestors. They express positive, almost sentimental attitudes toward their traditional culture, although this expression may be as much a function of the fact that it is the "right" thing to do as it is of a genuine concern for and involvement in the preservation of their heritage. Although there may be an interest in hearing or reading about old ethnic practices, the "new ethnics" do not subscribe to them. Removed temporarily and culturally from their immigrant forebears, they take a distant and detached view of their ethnicity. They stand back, outside of it so to speak, and ask, "Which aspects are important to me?" The "New Ethnicity", thus, is much more conscious, voluntary and rationalistic than the earlier ethnicity. In this variant, then, ethnicity is not a permanently inscribed status; it is something which can be resurrected or submerged as situational exigencies dictate. It is transitory and is manifested in activities requiring little commitment. Its form, thus is likely to be quite different from that characteristic of early-generation and working class ethnics.

For the latter, self-identity, recollection of the past and uniquely ethnic attitudes and behavior[107] were unproblematic because of the all-encompassing nature of early socialization experiences and associations later on in life. The unconscious adoption of ethnic values and behaviors, such as political styles, drinking habits or views of outsiders, could be sustained only as long as the ethnic social structure was intact. Today, however, continuous involvement in the cultural and social life of the community is not required to maintain ethnic awareness, which is a personal matter and is coming to be the major characteristic of the "New Ethnicity". Because of the emphasis on the subjective aspect of ethnicity, the objective condition of being of ethnic descent is less important than it used to be. What is more significant is the social-psychological component: a mind-set stressing ethnic pride and placing a positive valuation on in-group membership. Since there is little need today to interact on an ethnic basis, ethnic identity is neither deeply engrained nor long lasting and its present form may more correctly be termed a "label" than an "identity". Furthermore, because ethnic groups are now dispersed geographically and socioeconomically and because cultural, as well as structural, assimilation have advanced to the degree that they have, there is little pressure generated by the group itself to resist competing loyalties and identities,[108] thus, as Francis noted more than thirty years ago, it is not so much the disappearance or transformation of the factors that brought the group about which diminishes it as it is external conditions which provide alternative values and solidarities. So, rather than being a strongly felt psychological need, ethnicity and ethnic identification are particularly subject to exogenous influences and may be expected to wax and wane as external circumstances require.

Hence, one's sense of being an ethnic need not be implanted early in the socialization process for it to be present later in life. In this regard, ethnic intermarriage is significant, for marrying outside the group provides competing sources of identification within the family circle. Furthermore, because the common ethnic culture in a nuclear family in which the partners come from different nationality backgrounds is likely to be limited, it is probable that offspring will adopt an American identity, since it represents a common denominator. Although the process by which identifications are passed on from one generation to the next is complex and not yet understood, the ethnic integrity of the nuclear family may not be that crucial, even though it may be difficult to conceive, for example, of a person with a Scotch-Irish father and a

[108] *See,* Andrew M. Greeley, *Ethnicity in the United States.* New York: John Wiley and Sons, 1974. P. 310.

[108] E.K. Francis, "The Nature of the Ethnic Group", *American Journal of Sociology,* 52:398−400. March, 1947.

Polish-Italian mother thinking of himself as any of these. Perhaps the phenomenon is not so incomprehensible, given the legitimation of ethnicity today and the fact that it may even be considered fashionable to be an ethnic. So, although one did not start out as an ethnic, he can quite easily become one if he wishes because ethnicity today is more a state of mind than total immersion in the culture and communal life of the group, as it was in the past. What is needed to initiate and to sustain this kind of identificational ethnicity are symbolic activities, occasional reminders of one's ethnic descent: pasting a flag decal on the car, marching in or viewing a parade, celebrating a festival, travelling to the homeland, attending a lecture.[109] For these groups having a strong sense of attachment to the homeland, such as the Jews, events there may furnish suitable symbols. One's surname is certainly important because it is likely to influence how one is labelled by others, especially in a society emphasizing impersonal relationships, where little, except external trappings, are known by others. It would seem, thus, that only those aspects of ethnicity meeting the current needs of ethnics for discovering or renewing their roots with minimal commitment will continue. In the end, social relationships within the group may not be that crucial for sustaining the "New Ethnicity" and can be expected to diminish, as long as society continues to tolerate and promote ethnic diversity.

THE "NEW ETHNICITY" AND ITALIAN AMERICANS

THE new style of ethnicity means profound changes in the Italian community. Although strong family ties are likely to continue in the form of close and emotional attachments to kin, especially nuclear family members, mobility concerns will surpass the extended family in importance. There will be fewer opportunities for face-to-face contact and only infrequent occasions, such as summer vacations or holiday visitations, when close feelings can be strengthened through direct involvement in the family circle. The greatest alteration is likely to occur within the nuclear family itself. There will be less sex role segregation as more common interests between husband and wife develop due to similar socialization and education experiences. As ties to extend kin recede in significance, relationships among nuclear family members will grow and consist of deeper involvement with and

---

[109] Herbert Gans, "Symbolic Ethnicity: The Future of Ethnic Groups and Culture in America". In *On the Making of Americans: Essays in Honor of David Reisman.* Edited by Herbert Gans *etal.* Pennsylvania: University of Pennsylvania Press, 1979.

dependence on each other. This also means that there will be more reaching out to persons beyond the family — friends, neighbors, professionals — who are not likely to be Italian. The greater religiosity of the middle-class Italian also helps to solidify the family in as much as church-going becomes a family, rather than an exclusively female, activity.

Except for traditional Italian neighborhoods in larger urban centers, which continue to receive substantial numbers of new immigrants, the "Little Italies" which have dotted the urban landscape in most American cities since the turn of the century will experience a reduction in size and in their ability to instill in the younger members a commitment to the Italian culture and social structure. There is less internal differentiation in the Italian enclaves today, as the old town and village identities have broken down and Italians are discovering that their problems transcend provincial and even ethnic lines. Because a large percentage of residents are working class and have working class concerns, there will be conflict with other ethnic groups and minorities on the borders of the neighborhood as well as in other institutional spheres such as occupational, political and educational. Some Italians, mainly middle-class, will continue to move to the greener pastures of suburbia to escape the confining ethnic environment, as well as to avoid high taxes and the threat of integration. For these families, the right home at the right price, not a desire to live near other Italians, is the major factor in selecting a neighborhood. For those who remain in the central city, predominantly working-class Italians, there will continue to be the problems associated with being a blue-collar worker cited earlier. Such persons will provide fertile ground for the activities of community organizers, who will utilize ethnicity as a positive force for neighborhood preservation, and for politicians with the ability to link the coincident concerns of ethnicity and working-class status.

Those organizations not meeting the demands of the "New Ethnicity" as sources of symbolic attachment will diminish in importance. The clubs descendant from the early mutual aid societies are an example. Their original function of insurance and sociability is now exclusively the latter, but even here change is evident. Although the only requirements are to pay dues and to attend an occasional social affair, membership is declining as surrounding neighborhoods of unassimilated ethnics diminish. Evening drinks with fellow Italians at these clubs is a thing of the past. Such associations may survive as social institutions on a working-class basis but then, of course, they are Italian organizations in name only. Even new arrivals generally do not join because they do not live in the neighborhood and are better educated, which means they look to non-working-class organizations to satisfy their needs.

Other institutions, those not requiring active participation or deep commitment, are likely to survive and even to fourish. Organizations which can combine ethnicity with another interest, such as health and athletic-related activities, are a case in point. The club whose flavor is Italian — food, dances, trips — and which, on a regular basis, offers services and facilities, such as a gym, sauna or lunch, to non-ethnics, will succeed. This is so because it appeals to Italians and non-Italians alike: to the former, mainly because it is organized around the ethnic factor and, to the latter, because it satisfies social and recreational needs. In as much as this type of organization is a middle-class one and interferes little with other areas of living, its chances for continued viability are good.

Another type of organization whose future appears bright has the major function of service to the community, which is accomplished through the conscious preservation of ethnic heritage. By sponsoring lectures, readings, scholarships, etc., of course, the appeal is mostly to a middle-class, Italian audience, but includes others as well. At any rate, these associations are likely to prosper, not only because there are more Italians with money, interest and the desire for symbolic activities to satisfy identificational needs, but also because society says it is alright. Furthermore, women can take a more active role, a departure from earlier times when organizational participation was solely a male prerogative.

Faced with the movement out of surrounding neighborhoods by traditional parishioners, the Italian national parish may be expected to experience further decline in the coming decades. There are several reasons for this. For early Italians, church attendance and support were predominantly female activities. At about the time that the Italian male became involved in organized religion, he also joined the middle-class and moved to a neighborhood with other middle-class families. Furthermore, those who have moved away from the ethnic church have not been replaced, as recent immigrants have settled in outlying areas and joined churches there. Most importantly, Italian Catholicism has not recovered from the effects of its pre- and early-immigration experiences. The traditional anti-clerical feeling, which was so strong 75 years ago that a young man who showed an interest in the priesthood risked being disowned by his family, limited the number of priests of Italian descent. Consequently, the Italian American priest has not enjoyed the stature, say, that a Polish American priest has had in his parish. The early Italian was attached to religion (feasts, festivals, superstition), not to the church, a fact which could not be understood by the Irish clergy. Today, such a misunderstanding is less prevalent, as Irish dominance has declined and Italian religion is less characteristically Italian. Furthermore, those Italians who want to, the relatively unassimilated, can have an Italian priest and the others, those who have moved to suburbia, do not care. The relationship between the Irish Catholic Church and the Italian community is likely to shift from one of lack of comprehension to one of conflict over who controls the organization at the lower and middle levels. The power struggle will not involve parishioners, who will not see it; it will occur within the church hierarchy itself, as Italian priests seek to wrest power from the entrenched Irish prelates, a scene played many times before in diverse institutional settings with actors of other ethnic persuasions.

In the end, however, it is the symbols of Italian descent, rather than the traditional social structure, which are the hallmarks of the "New Ethnicity". The display of the Italian flag decal on one's automobile signifies awareness of and pride in national descent, although it is interesting to note that the flag of Italy has never been the object of reverence that it is in this country. Events in the homeland in general show little promise of stirring ethnic emotions in the United States, in as much as an Italian national identity is a recent phenomenon and did not exist among the ancestors of contemporary Italian Americans. An incident such as the slaying of Aldo Moro may evoke outrage, not so much because of the death of a national and political leader but rather as a reaction to the rise of Communism, and does little to enhance ethnic solidarity in the United States. Personnages, however, such as athletes, entertainers, politicians and saints are a ready source of ethnic pride. Indeed, saints seem ideally suited as symbols of Italian descent, for they combine the person-orientation and predilection for religious festival characteristic of Italians, with the demands of the "New Ethnicity" and the achievement of a national identity by Italians in the United States. Hence, the celebration of the feast of San Gennaro may do more to rekindle ethnic pride and to increase ethnic solidarity than any other single event, including Columbus Day, and may be considered *the* religious and secular holiday of Italian Americans, perhaps having the same significance Saint Patrick's Day holds for the Irish.

---

[110] *See*, Herbert Gans, *The Urban Villagers*. New York: The Free Press, 1962. Chapter 4.

THE FUTURE OF ETHNICITY

BY categorizing the "New Ethnicity" as centering around identificational and symbolic needs and whose major behavioral manifestation is an interest in one's heritage, I do not mean to imply that ethnicity is dead. Rather, I am emphasizing the continuously changing face of ethnicity and that national origin matters less and less as generations pass. Assimilation must be understood as a process, perhaps one that cannot be described as ever being completed. It may be that ethnicity will always matter to some degree and that the description of the "New Ethnicity" here is the "final" state, although this proposition is certainly speculative, as it is impossible to specify how long ethnicity can survive in its present form.

Despite the historical decline in the vitality of ethnicity, one cannot deny that today there is a resurgence of sorts, as manifested in the increased number of ethnically oriented journals, festivals and mass media appeals to hyphenated Americans to remember that they have two heritages. Some observers of the present scene, such as Andrew Greeley and Michael Novak, say that such ethnic viability, and the diversity and pluralism which it implies, is a good thing, although the extent of such a return may have been overemphasized in the attempt to refute prevailing ethnic stereotypes. Moreover, the revival appears to be an intellectual one, characteristic of highly educated persons who take an interest in their country of origin, read about it, attend a lecture, maybe even visit their ancestral homeland. Such persons, imbued with the spirit of the "New Ethnicity", do not automatically feel closer emotional attachment to their relatives or assume a fatalistic frame of mind or abandon old friends in favor of fellow ethnics, although they might search out others who have also rediscovered their ethnicity. Thus, the so-called revival involves primarily an increased interest but minimal participation in ethnicity, as Hansen suggested several decades ago.[111]

Hence, the ethnic resurgence is not a reversal of the assimilatory trend and at most is a detour on the road to a more complete assimilation. A combination of nostalgia, legitimation of ethnic diversity and the recently arrived intellectual's attribution of their own ethnic pride and identity to their fellow ethnics has created the illusion of a widespread rediscovery of ethnicity. In reality, however, the revival is a middle-class, largely symbolic and intellectual phenomenon, the major explanation of which is the fact that the descendants of the "new

[111] Marcus Lee Hansen, "The Third Generation in America", *Commentary*, 14:492–500. Nov., 1952.

immigration" immigrants are now moving into the middle-class *en masse* and doing those things which middle-class people generally do: read, travel, participate in cultural activities. While middle-class people attend lectures, subscribe to journals, etc., involvement in these activities is determined by the prevailing climate of opinion, which favors ethnic considerations, for working-class ethnics, even though of the third or fourth generation, generally are not concerned with these kinds of matters.

The revival is due more to societal legitimation than to factors intrinsic to the ethnic group, as the same effect is evident in may groups differing in various respects — time of arrival, size, class composition, etc. In the absence of such legitimation, the same phenomenon would probably occur, but would be less prevalent. Prejudice, at least of the overt variety, has virtually disappeared. The feeling of embarassment because of ethnic beginnings has subsided to the point where "Kiss me, I'm Italian" buttons proclaim pride in ethnic descent. The wearing of ethnicity on the lapel may be a phenomenon which recurs every so often, in as much as the seed of rekindling is ever-present. This is so because the fact of being of immigrant stock cannot be changed; therefore, ethnic awareness may lie dorment for awhile, to be reawakened periodically in successive generations as societal conditions demand. It is impossible to speculate how long these ethnic badges will continue to be sported unashamedly. One may recall that during the 1950s there was a widespread belief that a religious revival, which proved to be of short duration, was occurring. The ethnic revival of the 1970s may follow the same course.

The Questionnaire

THIS appendix provides the reader with a complete list of the questions utilized in the study and; provides the reader with the source of these questions so that he might compare the results of this study to those conducted by others.

Lettered notes to various questions in the questionnaire indicate works on which the questions were based.

The Questionnaire

1. How do you think of yourself, as an _____ Italian
   _____ Italian American
   _____ American
   _____ Other (Specify)

2. Do you or your spouse cook Italian dishes, besides spaghetti or pizza? Which ones?
   How often do you have any kind of Italian dish at home?
   Do you make your own pasta?

3. Do you speak Italian?   Do you read Italian?[j]

4. Do you think that there is a great deal of prejudice against Italians in this country?

5. What part of Italy are your ancestors from?

6. There are many groups in America. I would like to get your feelings toward some of them. Below is a diagram of a thermometer. It is a feeling thermometer because it measures your feelings toward these groups. Here's how it works. If you don't feel particularly warm or cold toward a group, then you would give it a meter reading in the middle, at the 50 degree mark. If you feel favorable toward a group, you would place it somewhere between 50 and 100 degrees, depending on how warm your feeling is toward the group. On the other hand, if you don't care for a group too much, then the meter reading would be somewhere between 0 and 50 degrees.

Protestant	——	100	Middle-class Italians	——
Italian	——	90	Upper-class Italians	——
German	——		Lower-class Italians	——
Japanese	——	80	Working-class Italians	——
Jew	——	70	Working-class blacks	——
Swede	——	60	Lower-class Irish	——
Polish	——	50	Upper-class Jews	——
Black	——		Middle-class Jews	——
Puerto Rican	——	40	Lower-class blacks	——
Mexican	——	30	Upper-class Irish	——
American Indian	——	20	Working-class Polish	——
Sicilian	——	10	Upper-class Protestants	——
Irish	——	0	Working Class Protestants	
			Middle-class Polish	
			Middle-class Protestants [c,d]	

7. Think of the friends you had when you were 17 or 18. How many were Italian?

_____More than half

_____About half

_____Less than half

_____None

8. Think of your three closest friends today. Provide the following information for each: sex, nationality, religion, occupation, age, how long known, how often in contact, how many of the other does each know well?

9. Think of the other friends you have today. How many of them are Italian? How many of them have the same religion as you? How many belong to the same class as you?

_____More than half   _____Less than half

_____About half   _____None

10. Think of the friends you visit with most often. Are these the same your spouse will visit with most often?

11. Are you still living in the neighborhood where you grew up or close to it?

_____Same neighborhood

_____Close to it

_____Not living in or close to it

12. How many of the people in the neighborhood in which you were raised were Italian?

_____ More than half

_____ About half

_____ Less than half

_____ None

13. How many people at the church that you attend are Italian?

    _____ More than half
    _____ About half
    _____ Less than half
    _____ None

14. What is the nationality and religion of the following persons with whom you deal most frequently? Doctor, Dentist, Lawyer, Clergyman

15. Which organizations do you presently belong to? How active are you in each?

16. Do you belong to any club or organization which attracts mainly Italians? What is the name of it?

17. Are there any problems in the community in which mostly Italians are on one side and another group on the other side?
What is this problem?
Have you done anything to support the Italian side?
What was it?

18. Have you ever worked with any other organization in this community to try to solve some community problems?
How many of the other people who belong to this organization are Italian?

    _____More than half
    _____About half
    _____Less than half
    _____None

19. Have you ever done work for one of the major political parties or candidates?   For whom did you work?   What did you do?

20. How much of the time do you think you can trust the local government to do what is right?

    _____Always
    _____Most of the time
    _____Some of the time
    _____None of the time

21. How much of the time do you think you can trust the government in Washington to do what is right?

    _____Always
    _____Most of the time
    _____Some of the time
    _____None of the time[c]

22. In general, which of the following attitudes do you think a person should take toward new neighbors:

_____Go over to their house after they move in and offer help

_____Go over to their house and introduce yourself, but do not offer help unless they ask for it.

_____Don't go over unless invited, but be friendly.

_____Don't become too friendly until you have had some time to to see what kind of people they are.

_____Stay away from all newcomers and keep to life-time friends.

23. Should divorce in this country be easier, more difficult or as difficult to obtain as it is now?[a]

24. Please tell me whether or not you think it should be possible for a pregnant woman to obtain a legal abortion if:

There is a strong chance of serious defect in the baby.

She is married and does not want any more children

The woman's own health is seriously endangered by the pregnancy

She became pregnant as a result of rape

She is not married and does not want to marry the man[a]

25. On an average weekday, how much time do you and your spouse spend together in conversation?

_____Less than an hour

_____One hour

_____Two hours

_____Three hours or more

26. How do you or would you discipline your young child if he or she disobeyed you?

27. Who usually does the following, husband or wife?

Straightens up the living room when company is coming.

Supermarket shopping.

The evening dishes.

Keeps track of the money and bills.

Repairs things around the house.

Keeps in touch with wife's relatives.

Keeps in touch with husband's relatives.

Mows the lawn.

The cooking.

Talks to children's teachers.

POSSIBLE ANSWERS: Wife always, Wife more than Husband, Husband and Wife the same. Husband more than Wife, Husband always.[1]

Who usually makes the final decision regarding the following?

What job husband should take.

What car to buy.

Whether or not to buy life insurance.

Where to go on vacation.

What house or apartment to take.

Whether or not wife should go to work or quit work.

What doctor to have when someone is sick.

How much to spend per week on food.

What to do on Saturday night.

> POSSIBLE ANSWERS: Wife always, Wife more than husband, Husband and wife the same, Husband more than wife, Husband always.[i]

28. How often, in the past two weeks, have you and your spouse done each of the following things together?

Visited your relatives.

Visited your spouse's relatives.

Ate out at a restaurant

Played with your children

Went to a movie.

Talked about husband's work.

29. Would you move out of the Bridgeport area if you or your husband got an offer of a better job, even if it meant less contact with friends and relatives?

30. Think of the five persons that you feel closest to.

> How many of the five are relatives of yours?
> How many of the five are relatives of your spouse?
> How many of the five are friends of yours or your spouse?

31. Below is a list of relatives. How close do you feel to each one or group? Mother, Father, Grandparents, Brothers, Sisters, Married Children, Aunts, Uncles, Cousins, In-Laws.

> POSSIBLE ANSWERS: Very close, Pretty close, Not too close, Not close at all, Not alive or do not have any.

32. Have you experienced any discrimination in: Getting a house or apartment? Getting a job? Getting a promotion?

33. Listed below are a number of nationality groups. Consider each nationality group one at a time and indicate the closest relation you have with each. Irish, Protestant, German, Jewish, Swedish,

Polish, Negro, Puerto-Rican, Mexican, Japanese, Chinese, American Indian.

POSSIBLE ANSWERS: Relative, Best Friend, Close Friend, Friend, Neighbor, Co-worker, Knew in school, Acquaintance, Stranger.

34. Please respond to the questions below by putting a number, from 1 to 6, in the slot next to each statement. The numbers range from 1 (strongly agree) to 6 (strongly disagree), as indicated in the following scale:

1	2	3	4	5	6
Strongly Agree	Agree	Mildly Agree	Mildly Disagree	Disagree	Strongly Disagree

The government in Washington is trying to do too many things that should be left to individuals and private businesses.[c]

A person who is an admitted Communist should not be allowed to make a speech in this community.[a]

A person who is against all churches and religion should not be allowed to make a speech in this community.[a]

A boy should be tough and aggressive.

A child should never be allowed to talk back to his parents or it will lose respect for them.[h]

Even if a woman has the ability and interest, she should not choose a career field that will be difficult to combine with bringing up children. [b]

Parents should encourage just as much independence in their daughters as in their sons.[b,f]

Young people should seek the consent of their parents in deciding whom to marry.

A good girl is one who is quiet and shy.

There are times when it is necessary to spank a child to make him behave.

We fool ourselves if we think we can control the course of our own lives.[b]

God is a personal being who listens to my prayers and sometimes answers them.

The best way to judge a man is by his seccess in his occupation.[e]

All a young man should want out of a career is a secure, not too difficult job with enough pay to afford a nice car and eventually a home of his own.[e]

It is important to me that my children marry someone of my own class.

Planning only makes a person unhappy, since your plans hardly ever work out anyway.[e]

One's job should come first, even if it means sacrificing time from recreation.[e]

Most people can't be trusted and if you don't watch out they will take advantage of you.[f]

White people have a right to keep Negroes out of their neighborhoods if they want and Negroes should respect that right.[f,g]

A person suspected of armed robbery should be kept in jail without bail to prevent him from committing any crime while he is waiting for his trial.

The public schools should teach more about the contributions of Italian people to America.[k]

I feel more comfortable in an Italian church.[k]

We don't need stronger organizations to express the views of Italian Americans.[k]

An Italian neighborhood is a friendlier place to live.[k]

Organizations which carry on the Italian culture are important.[k]

Italian religious education is not important for our children.[k]

Italian music makes me want to dance.[k]

Our people should get their families to the Italian church on Sundays.[k]

You should belong to the Italian church even if it is far from your home.[k]

Is it alright to change your name so that it will not be taken for Italian.[j,k]

I feel more comfortable with Italian people.[k]

It is important to me that my children marry someone of my own nationality.[k]

We don't need to know the history of the Italian people.[k]

I would rather attend an Italian Mass at Christmas.[k]

Italian jokes bother me.[k]

It is important for me to contribute my time, talent and finance to the Italian church.[k]

If you're in trouble, you cannot count on Italian people to help you.[k]

We would be willing to give money to preserve the Italian tradition.[k]

I should not encourage others to belong to the Italian church.[k]

Our children should learn Italian dance and music.[k]

I prefer a church where services are in the Italian language.[k]

It is too bad that the Italian tradition is not being carried on by many of our young people.[k]

I would vote for an Italian political candidate rather than any other nationality regardless of political party.[k]

Our children should learn to speak Italian.[k]

You can be for your own people first and still be a good American.[k]

It is important for me to help Italians who have just come over from Italy to adapt to the American way of life.

Italian politicians can't be trusted any more than other politicians can.[k]

I have a right to question what my church teaches.

It is important to me that my children marry someone of their own religion.

I would rather visit with my friends than with my relatives.

The Bible is God's work and all it says is true.

35. Please list all persons who presently live in this household (include unmarried children at school) and indicate their age, sex, marital status and relation to you.

36. What is your main occupation now? (If unemployed, what is your occupation when you are working?)

    What was your first full-time job?

37. What is your spouse's main occupation now?

    What was your spouse's first full-time job?

38. What is or was the main occupation of your father?

    What is or was the main occupation of your spouse's father?

39. What is your religion? Were you raised in this religion? If no, what religion were you raised in?

    When were you converted?

40. What is your spouse's religion? Was he/she raised in this religion? If no, what religion was he/she raised in?

    When was he/she converted?

39. What is your religion? Were you raised in this religion? If no, what religion were your raised in?

    When were you converted?

41. About how often have you attended religious services in the past year?

About how often has your spouse attended religious services in the past year?

          _____Once a week or more

          _____Two or three times a month

          _____Once a month

          _____A few times a year or less

          _____Never

42. What is the main reason you attend religious services?

          _____Because I've always gone

          _____To meet my friends

          _____Family or friends expect it

          _____To worship God or pray

          _____God expects it

          _____To hear sermon

          _____To learn how to be a better person

          _____To make me feel better

          _____Other (specify)

43. What is your mother's religion? What is your father's religion?

44. What is your spouse's mother's religion?
    What is your spouse's father's religion?

45. What religion are you raising your children in?

46. What is the highest grade you have completed in school?
    Have you ever attended parochial school?
    If yes, how many years did you complete in parochial school at each of the following levels? Elementary, High School, College.

47. What is the highest grade your spouse completed in school?
    Did he/she ever attend parochial school?
    If yes, how many years did he/she complete in parochial school at each of the following levels? Elementary, High School, College.

48. Do you consider yourself a? Democrat, Republican, Independent, Other.

49. Do you own or rent your home?
    How long have you lived in the Bridgeport area?
    How long has your spouse lived in the Bridgeport area?
    How many people in the neighborhood in which you now live are Italian?

          _____More than half

          _____About half

          _____Less than half

          _____None

50. How long have you been married?
   Have you ever been married before?   If yes, for how long?
   ˙ Has your spouse ever been married before? If yes, for how long?

51. How many children do you have now? (Include married children)
   How many would you like to have altogether?
   How many would your spouse like to have altogether?

52. Which social class do you belong to?
   _____Upper
   _____Middle
   _____Working
   _____Lower

53. Into which of the following categories does your total annual
   family income from all sources (before taxes) fall? Include only
   yours and your spouse's; do not include earnings from any other
   person in your household.

$0 — $ 2,499	$12,500 — $14,999
$ 2,500 — $ 4,999	$15,000 — $17,499
$ 5,000 — $ 7,499	$17,500 — $19,999
$ 7,500 — $ 9,999	$20,000 — $24,999
$10,000 — $12,499	$25,000 or above

54. What is the nationality of your mother?
   What is the nationality of your father?

   Were you born in this country?
   Was your mother born in this country?
   Was your father born in this country?
   How many grandparents were born in this country?

55. What is the nationality of your spouse's mother?
   What is the nationality of your spouse's father?

   Was your spouse born in this country?
   Was your spouse's mother born in this country?
   Was your spouse's father born in this country?
   How many of your spouse's grandparents were born in this country?

[a] National Opinion Research Center (NORC) General Social Survey — Spring, 1976.

[b] NORC College Graduate Survey — March, 1964 — Survey # 483.

[c] NORC — December, 1973 — Survey # 41790.

[d] NORC — Education and Values in America — February, 1974 — Survey # 4172.

[e] NORC — June, 1965 — Survey # 466.

[f] NORC November, 1972 — Survey # 5046.

[g] NORC — April, 1970 — Survey # 4100.

[h] NORC — March, 1971 — Survey # 4119.

[i] Robert O. Blood and Donald M. Wolfe. *Husbands and Wives*. New York: The Free Press. 1960.

[j] Patrick J. Gallo. *Ethnic Alienation*. Rutherford, New Jersey: Fairleigh Dickinson University press. 1974.

[k] Neil Sandberg, *Ethnic Identity and Assimilation: The Polish American Community. New York*: Praeger: 1974.

APPENDIX B

The Demography of the Two Subsamples

An examination of Table B.1 indicates little differentiation between the two subsamples which have been combined to form the data base for the analysis contained in this study. The respondents in the non-random sample are slightly younger, have less Italian parentage and are more heavily represented in the more-than-sixteen-years-of-schooling and professional, technical occupational categories than their counterparts in the random subsample. The largest difference between the two subsamples is the distribution on the sex variable: 30 percent of the respondents in the random sample and 52 percent of those in the non-random sample are female. An analysis of the relationship between sex and the measures of assimilation revealed that being male or female makes little difference in terms of the subprocesses which were studied.

Table B.1

The Demography of the Two Subsamples

	Random Sample	Non-Random Sample
GENERATION		
R born in Italy	5%	7%
R born in U.S., 2 parents born in Italy	46	40
R and 1 pt. born in U.S.	19	25
R and 2 pts. born in U.S.	22	18
R and 1+ grandparents born in U.S.	8	10
	100% N=339	100% N=128
AGE		
60+ Years	16%	19%
50 — 59 Years	26	23
40 — 49 Years	28	22
30 — 39 Years	20	21
20 — 29 Years	10	15
	100% N=341	100% N=128
PARENTAGE		
2 Parents Italian	85%	81%
1 Parent Italian	15	19
	100% N=341	100% N=128

TABLE B.1 (continued)
The Demography of the Two Subsamples

	Random Sample	Non-Random Sample
EDUCATION		
0–8 Grades	7%	7%
9–11 Grades	14	13
H.S. Graduate	39	39
13–15 Grades	14	17
College Graduate	15	7
16+ Grades	11	17
	100% N=334	100% N=128
OCCUPATION		
Unskilled Blue Collar	19%	22%
Skilled Blue Collar	16	6
Sales, Clerical	20	24
Proprietors	7	7
Mgrs., Admstrs.	15	10
Prof., Tech.	23	31
	100% N=293	100% N=107
SEX		
Male	70%	48%
Female	30	52
	100% N=341	100% N=128

APPENDIX C

SUPPLEMENTARY TABLES

Table C.1

Tau Measurements between Background
Variables and Measures of Distrust of Others

	Attitudes Toward New Neighbors	Generalized Mistrust
Generation	.06*	.08*
Parentage	.13*	.03
Age	.07*	.03
Education	− .09*	− .12*
Occupation	− .04	− 10*
Income	− .02	− .09*

NOTE: Significant at .05 level.

Table C.2

Distribution of Responses to Cultural Heritage Statements[a]

ITEM	Strongly Agree	Agree	Mildly Agree	Mildly Disagree	Disagree	Strongly Disagree	Total (N)
1. Schools should teach about Italian contributions.	10%	22%	29%	15%	23%	1%	100% (452)
2. Italian cultural organizations are important.	17	49	21	4	8	1	100% (455)
3. Italian music makes me dance.	17	39	18	7	15	4	100% (453)
4. Italians should know Italian history.	17	42	23	8	8	2	100% (453)
5. Italians should give money to preserve Italian tradition.	6	21	25	18	23	7	100% (451)
6. Children should know Italian dances and music.	8	21	30	15	21	5	100% (445)
7. Children should carry on Italian traditions.	13	34	22	11	15	5	100% (453)
8. Children should speak Italian.[b]	16	35	27	7	12	3	100% (455)

Table C.2 (continued)
Distribution of Responses to Cultural Heritage Statements[a]

NOTES:

[a] These statements are based on similar ones used by Sandberg (1974) in the construction of his group cohesiveness scale.

[b] The actual statements are:

1. The public schools should teach more about the contributions of Italian people to America.

2. Organizations which carry on the Italian culture are important.

3. Italian music makes me want to dance.

4. We don't need to know the history of the Italian people. (Note that the statement has been reworded in the table in order that all "agree" responses represent support for the Italian position.)

5. You should be willing to give money to preserve the Italian tradition.

6. Our children should learn Italian dances and music.

7. It is too bad that the Italian tradition is not being carried on by many of our young people.

8. Our children should learn to speak Italian.

Table C.3

Distribution of Responses to Religious Cultural Statements[a]

ITEM	Strongly Agree	Agree	Mildly Agree	Mildly Disagree	Disagree	Strongly Disagree	Total (N)
1. Feel more comfortable in an Italian church.	6%	8%	9%	14%	49%	14%	100% (449)
2. Should belong to Italian church.	2	4	5	13	56	20	100 (448)
3. Prefer services in Italian language	1	3	4	17	53	22	100 (448)
4. Prefer Italian Mass at Christmas	6	14	11	15	42	12	100 (449)
5. Italian religious education is important for children	5	23	20	15	33	4	100 (439)
6. Important to aid Italian church.	2	7	9	15	50	17	100 (441)
7. Should encourage others to belong to Italian church.	11	25	13	15	29	7	100 (437)
8. Families should attend Italian church.[b]	5	11	11	17	46	10	100 (446)

NOTES:

a These statements are based on similar ones used by Sandberg (1974) in the construction of his group cohesiveness scale.

b The actual statements are:

1. I feel more comfortable in an Italian church.

2. You should belong to the Italian church even if it is far from your home.

3. I prefer a church where services are in the Italian language.

4. I would rather attend an Italian Mass at Christmas.

5. Italian religious education is not important for our children. (Note that this statement has been reworded in the table so that all "agree" responses represent support for the Italian position.)

6. It is important for me to contribute my time, talent, and finances to the Italian church.

7. I should not encourage others to belong to the Italian church. (See note for Statement No. 5 above.)

8. Our people should get their families to the Italian church on Sundays.

Table C.4

Tau Measurements between Ethno-Religious Characteristics
of Professional Service Personnel and Background Variables

	Doctor	Dentist	Lawyer	Clergyman
Generation	.05	.07	.16*	.01
Parentage	.07*	.05	.11*	.03
Age	.01	.01	.03	.00
Education	.02	-.04	-.02	-.01
Occupation	-.01	.00	-.07	-.03
Income	-.08	.02	-.06	-.09

NOTE: * Significant at .05 level.

Table C.5

Tau Measurements between Early Environment
and Measures of Primary and Secondary Association

	Neighborhood	Adolescent Friendship Group
Secondary Associations		
Belong to Italian Organization	.03	.08*
Doctor — Ethno-Religious Homogeneity	.01	.00
Dentist — Ethno-Religious Homogeneity	.02	.11*
Lawyer — Ethno-Religious Homogeneity	.04	.06
Clergyman — Ethno-Religious Homogeneity	.15*	.09*
Primary Associations		
How Close Feel To:		
Mother	.03	.01
Father	.03	.11
Grandparents	.12	-.11
Brother(s)	.07	.07
Sister(s)	.05	.08
Married Children	-.05	.06
Aunts	.08*	.08*
Uncles	.08*	.08*
Cousins	.04	.10
Inlaws	.01	-.01
Three Closest Friends Italian	.15*	.29*
Three Closest Friends Same Religion	.06	.17*
Three Closest Friends Same Census		
Occupational Category	-.03	-.08*
Wider Friendship Group — Same Ethnicity	.27*	.43*
Wider Friendship Group — Same Religion	.21*	.27*
Wider Friendship Group — Same Class	.08*	.11*

NOTE: * Significant at .05 level.

Table C.6

Percentage of Respondents Feeling That
There is a Great Deal of Prejudice Against
Italians by Background Variables

	Percentage	
Generation		
R born in Italy	25%	
R born in U.S., 2 parents born in Italy	33	
R and 1 parent born in U.S.	26	
R and 2 parents born in U.S.	16	
R and 1+ grandparents born in U.S.	18	N = 459
Age*		
60+ Years	29%	
50—59	37	
40—49	25	
30—39	14	
20—29	22	N = 462
Occupation		
Unskilled Blue Collar	35%	
Skilled Blue Collar	28	
Sales, Clerical	22	
Proprietors	29	
Managers, Administrators	24	
Professional, Technical	21	N = 392
Parentage		
2 Parents Italian	28%	
1 Parent Italian	16	N = 456
Education		
0—8 Grades	24%	
9—11 Grades	29	
H.S. Graduate	29	
13—15 Grades	28	
College Graduate	27	
16+ Grades	14	N = 454

Note: * Significant at .05 level.

Table C.7

Measures of Structural Assimilation
by Measures of Assimilation in Other Areas

| | Of 5 Persons Closest To | | 3 Closest Friends | | | | | |
| | | | Italian | | Same Religion as R | | Same Census Occupational Category | |
	0–2 are Friends	3–5 are Friends	2–3	0–1	2–3	0–1	2–3	0–1
CULTURAL[a]								
Language and Cooking Skills	43%	34%	58%*	33%	53%*	32%	31%	47%
Destiny Scale	53	49	56	55	58	54	51	59
Heritage Scale	50	52	62*	48	55*	49	53	54
Nationality Scale	49	41	60*	43	52	35	49	50
Religious Scale	43	46	57*	40	51*	34	50	47
IDENTIFICATIONAL[b]								
Ethnic Self Identity	67	66	82*	60	70*	56	64	69
MARITAL								
Ethnic Endogamy[c]	44	42	69*	46	48*	45	50	54
Religious Endogamy[d]	81	77	84	75	84*	58	80	77

Table C.7 (continued)
Measures of Structural Assimilation
by Measures of Assimilation in Other Areas

	Of 5 Persons Closest To		3 Closest Friends					
			Italian		Same Religion as R		Same Census Occupational Category	
	0–2 are Friends	3–5 are Friends	2–3	0–1	2–3	0–1	2–3	0–1
ATTITUDE AND BEHAVIOR RECEPTIONAL								
Prejudice[e]	27	16	30*	24	26	30	25	27
Discrimination[f]	6	3	7	4	6	3	2*	7
CIVIC								
Civic Scale[a]	52*	46	64	49	57	45	54	54
Abortion[g]	26	17	25	19	25*	9	22	10

NOTE: * Significant at .05 level.

a The figures are the percentages of respondents scoring high on the scale.

b The figures are the percentages of respondents who claim "Italian" or "Italian American" identity.

c The figures are the percentages of respondents who have both pairs of parents same ethnicity.

d The figures are the percentages of respondents who were raised in the same religion as their spouse.

e The figures are the percentages of respondents who feel that there is a great deal of prejudice against Italians.

f The figures are the percentages of respondents who report 2—3 cases of discrimination.

g The figures are the percentages of respondents who favor the legalization of abortion in 3 or more cases.

Table C.8

Matrix of Tau Measurements
between Measures of Assimilation[a]

	Ethnic Self Identity	Ethnic Endogamy	Religious Endogamy	Prejudice	Discrimination	Civic Scale	Abortion
CULTURAL ASSIMILATION							
Language and Cooking Skills Scale	.31*	.26*	.14*	.15*	.02	.16*	-.11*
Heritage Scale	.23*	.19*	.04	.18*	.13*	.21*	-.13*
Destiny Scale	.07*	.13*	.03	.06*	-.02	.27*	-.04
Nationality Scale	.19*	.15*	.02	.19*	.03	.23*	.08*
Religious Scale	.22*	.19*	-.05	.08*	-.01	.19*	-.06
IDENTIFICATIONAL							
Ethnic Self-Identity	—	.10*	.04	.07	.02	.12*	-.01
MARITAL							
Ethnic Endogamy	.10*	—	.24*	-.02	.00	.12*	.03
Religious Endogamy	.04	.24*	—	-.04	-.08*	.04	.03

Table C.8 (continued)

Matrix of Tau Measurements
between Measures of Assimilation[a]

	Ethnic Self Identity	Ethnic Endogamy	Religious Endogamy	Prejudice	Discrimination	Civic Scale	Abortion
ATTITUDE AND BEHAVIOR RECEPTIONAL							
Prejudice	.07	-.02	-.04	—	.11*	.02	-.06*
Discrimination	.02	.00	-.08*	.11*	—	-.07	.02
CIVIC							
Civic Scale	.12*	.12*	.04	.02	-.07	—	.04
Abortion	-.01	.03	.03	-.06*	.02	.04	—

Note: * Significant at .05 level.

[a] The fact that the Tau measurements are lower than expected is due to several factors. The computation of Tau involves a deduction for those instances in which two cases are tied in their relative ordering on two variables. Therefore, the magnitude of the relationship is less than it would be if a less powerful measure of association was used. Also, the degree of relationship is dependent on the number of values for each variable and the distribution of the cases across these values.

References and
Suggested Reading

Abramson, Harold, *Ethnic Diversity in Catholic America.* New York: John Wiley and Sons, 1973.

_____ "The Religioethnic Factor and the American Experience: Another Look at the Three-Generation Hypothesis", *Ethnicity,* 2:163—177. June, 1975.

Alba, Richard D., "Social Assimilation Among American Catholic National-Origin Groups", *American Sociological Review,* 41:1030—1046. Dec., 1976.

_____ "Ethnic Networks and Tolerant Attitudes", *Public Opinion Quarterly,* 42:1—16. Spring, 1978.

Amfitheatrof, Erik, *The Children of Columbus: An Informal History of Italians in the New World.* Boston: Little, Brown and Company, 1973.

Annals of the American Academy of Political and Social Science, "The New Immigration", Volume 367, September, 1966.

Banfield, Edward C., *The Moral Basis of a Backward Society,* New York: The Free Press, 1958.

Baroni, Geno M., "Ethnicity and Public Policy". In *Pieces of a Dream.* Edited by Michael Wenk, S.M. Tomasi and Geno Baroni. Staten Island: Center for Migration Studies, 1972.

Barzini, Luigi, *The Italians.* New York: Atheneum Press, 1964.

Bell, Daniel, "Ethnicity and Social Change". In *Ethnicity.* Edited by Nathan Glazer and Daniel F. Moynihan. Cambridge: Harvard University Press, 1975. Pp. 141—174.

Bender, Eugene and George Kagiwada, "Hansen's Law of Third-Generation Return and the Study of American Religio-Ethnic Groups", *Phylon,* 29:360—370. Winter, 1968.

Berkson, Isaac B., *Theories of Americanization: A Critical Study.* New York: Arno Press, 1969.

Bettelheim, Bruno and Morris Janowitz, *Social Change and Prejudice.* Glencoe, Illinois: The Free Press, 1964.

Blalock, Hubert M., *Social Statistics*. New York: McGraw-Hill, 1972.

Borhek, J.T., "Ethnic Group Cohesion", *American Journal of Sociology*, 76:33—46. July, 1970.

Breton, Raymond E. "Institutional Completeness of Ethnic Communities and the Personal Relations of Immigrants", *American Journal of Sociology*, 70:193—205. July, 1964.

Bugelski, B.R., "Assimilation Through Intermarriage", *Social Forces*, 40:148—153. Dec., 1961.

Bushee, Frederick O., "Italian Immigrants in Boston". In *A Documentary History of the Italian-Americans*. Edited by Wayne Moquin. New York: Praeger Press, 1974. Pp. 49—54.

Campisi, Paul J., "Ethnic Family Patterns: The Italian Family in the United States", *American Journal of Sociology*, 28:443—449. May, 1948.

Castiglione, G.E. DiPalma, "Italian Immigration into the United States, 1901—1904", *American Journal of Sociology*, 3:183—206. Sept., 1905.

Child, Irvin, *Italian or American*. New Haven: Yale University Press, 1943.

Cohen, Steven Martin, "Socioeconomic Determinants of Interethnic Marriage and Friendship", *Social Forces*, 55:997—1011. June, 1977.

Cohen, Steven Martin and R.E. Kapsis, "Religion, Ethnicity and Party Affiliation in the United States: Evidence from Pooled Electoral Surveys, 1968—1972", *Social Forces*, 56:637—653. Dec., 1977.

Cole, Stewart G. and Mildred Wiese, *Minorities and the American Promise.* New York: Harper and Brothers, 1954.

Cooley, Charles Horton, *Human Nature and Social Order*. New York: Scribner's, 1902.

Covello, Leonard, *The Social Background of the Italo-American School Child*. Leiden, Netherlands: E.J. Brill, 1967.

Dahl, Robert, *Who Governs?* New Haven: Yale University Press, 1961.

D'Alesandre, John Jr., *Occupational Trends of Italians in New York City*. New York: Casa Italiana Education Bureau, Bulletin No. 8, 1935.

Davenport, William E., "The Exodus of a Latin People", *Charities*, 12:463—467. May 7, 1904.

Drachsler, Julius, *Democracy and Assimilation*. New York: MacMillan Company, 1920.

Driedger, Leo, "Ethnic Self-Identity: A Comparison of In-Group Evaluations", *Sociometry*, 39:131—141. June, 1976.

Eisenstadt, S.N., *The Absorption of Immigrants*. London: Routledge and Kegan Paul, 1954.

——————— *The Absorption of Immigrants*. Glencoe, Illinois: The Free Press, 1955.

Eisinger, Peter K., "Ethnicity As a Strategic Option: An Emerging View", *Public Administration Review*, 38:89—93. Jan.—Feb., 1978.

Etzioni, Amital, "The Ghetto: A Re-evaluation", *Social Forces*, 37:255—262. Mar., 1959.

Fabian, Illona, *The Transformation of Culture and Knowledge and Emergence of Ethnicity Among Czech Immigrants in Chicago*. Unpublished Research Proposal. Department of Anthropology, University of Chicago, 1972.

Featherman, David, "The Socio-Economic Achievement of White Ethnic Subgroups: Social and Psychological Explanations", *American Sociological Review*, 36:207—222. Apr., 1971.

Feinstein, Otto, *Ethnic Groups in the City*. Lexington, Massachusetts: Heath Lexington Books, 1971.

Fishman, Joshua, "American Immigrant Groups", *Sociology Review*, 13:311—326. Nov., 1965.

Fishman, Joshua A., *etal., Language Loyalty in the United States*. The Hague: Mouton, 1966.

Foerster, Robert F., *The Italian Emigration of Our Times*. New York: Arno Press, 1969.

Francis, E.K., "The Nature of the Ethnic Group", *American Journal of Sociology*, 52:393—400. Mar., 1947.

——————, *Interethnic Relations: An Essay in Sociological Theory*. New York: Elsevier, 1976.

Fuchs, Lawrence, ed., *American Ethnic Politics*. New York: Harper and Row, 1968.

Gallo, Patrick. *Ethnic Alienation*. Cranbury, New Jersey: Fairleigh Dickinson University Press. 1974.

Gambino, Richard, *Blood of My Blood*. New York: Doubleday, 1974.

Gans, Herbert, "American Jewry: Present and Future", *Commentary*, 21:422—430. May, 1956.

—————— "American Jewry: Present and Future", *Commentary*. 21:555—563. June, 1956.

—————— *The Urban Villagers*. New York: The Free Press, 1962.

——————"Symbolic Ethnicity: The Future of Ethnic Groups and Cultures in America". In *On the Making of Americans: Essays in Honor of David Riesman*. Edited by H. Gans, H. Glazer, J. Gusfield and C. Jencks. Pennsylvania: University of Pennsylvania Press, 1979.

Glaser, Daniel, "Dynamics of Ethnic Identification", *American Sociological Review*, 23:31—40. Feb., 1958.

Glazer, Nathan, "Ethnic Groups in America". In *Freedom and Control in Modern Society*. Edited by Morroe Berger, Theodore Abel and Charles H. Page. New York: D. Van Nostrand Co., 1954. Pp. 158—173.

—————— "Slums and Ethnicity". In *Social Welfare and Urban Problems*. Edited by Thomas D. Sherrard. New York: Columbia University Press, 1971.

—————— "Who Do We Think We Are?", *Harvard Magazine*. Mar., 1974.

Glazer, Nathan and Daniel F. Moynihan, *Beyond the Melting Pot*. Cambridge: MIT Press, 1970.

—————————————————— "Why Ethnicity?", *Commentary*, 58:33—39. Oct., 1974.

Goering, John, "The Emerging of Ethnic Interests", *Social Forces*, 49:379—384. Mar., 1971.

Gordon, Milton M., *Assimilation in American Life*. New York: Oxford University Press, 1964.

─────────── "Toward a General Theory of Racial and Ethnic Group Relations". In *Ethnicity*. Edited by Nathan Glazer and Daniel P. Moynihan. Cambridge: Harvard University Press, 1975.

Greeley, Andrew M., *Why Can't They Be Like Us?* New York: Human Relations Press, 1969.

───────────, "Political Attitudes Among American White Ethnics", *Public Opinion Quarterly*, 36:213−220. Summer, 1972.

───────────, *Ethnicity in the United States*. New York: John Wiley and Sons, 1974.

───────────, "Political Participation Among Ethnic Groups in the United States", *American Journal of Sociology*, 80:170−204. July, 1974.

───────────, *Ethnicity, Denomination and Tranquility*. Beverly Hills, California: Sage Publications, 1976.

Greeley, Andrew M. and Peter H. Rossi, *The Education of Catholic Americans*. Chicago: Aldine, 1966.

Greer, Scott, "Catholic Voters and the Democratic Party", *Public Opinion Quarterly*, 25:611−625. Winter, 1961.

Handlin, Oscar, *The Uprooted*. New York: Grosset and Dunlap, 1951.

───────────, *Boston's Immigrants: A Study in Acculturation*. Cambridge: Harvard University Press, 1959.

Hensen, Marcus Lee, *The Immigrant in American History*. Cambridge: Harvard University Press, 1940.

───────────, "The Third Generation in America", *Commentary*, 14:492−500. Nov., 1952.

Heiss, Jerold, "Premarital Characteristics of the Religious Intermarried in an Urban Area", *American Sociological Review*, 25:47−55. Feb., 1960.

Herbert, Will, *Protestant, Catholic, Jew*. Garden City, New York: Doubleday and Co., 1955.

Higham, John, *Strangers in the Land: Patterns of American Nativism 1860−1925*. New York: Atheneum, 1965.

Hollingshead, August B., "Cultural Factors in the Selection of Marriage Mates", *American Sociological Review*, 15:619−627. Oct., 1950.

Hughes, Everett C., "Race Relations and the Sociological Imagination", *American Sociological Review*, 28:879−890. Dec., 1963.

Huchinson, E.P., *Immigrants and Their Children: 1850−1950*. New York: John Wiley and Sons, 1956.

Ianni, Francis. "The Italo-American Teenager". *The Annals, 338:70−78. Nov., 1961.*

Iorizzo, Luciano and Salvatore Mondello, *The Italian Americans*. New York: Twayne, 1971.

Jones, Maldwyn Allen, *American Immigration*. Chicago: The University of Chicago Press, 1960.

Kallen, Horace, "Democracy *Versus* the Melting Pot", *The Nation*, 100:190−194. Feb. 18, 1915.

───────────, "Democracy *Versus* the Melting Pot", *The Nation*, 100:217−220. Feb. 25, 1915.

───────────, *Culture and Democracy in the United States*. New York: Boni and Liveright, 1924.

Kantrowitz, Nathan, *Ethnic and Racial Segregation in the New York Metropolis: Residential Patterns Among White Ethnic Groups, Blacks, and Puerto Ricans.* New York: Praeger, 1973.

Keller, Suzanne, *The Urban Neighborhood.* New York: Random House, 1968.

Kennedy, Ruby Jo Reeves, "Single or Triple Melting Pot? Intermarriage Trends in New Haven", *American Journal of Sociology,* 49:331—339. Jan., 1944.

—————————, "Single or Triple Melting Pot? Intermarriage in New Haven, 1870—1950", *American Journal of Sociology,* 58:56—59. July, 1952.

Kornblum, William, *Blue Collar Community.* Chicago: University of Chicago Press, 1974.

Kourvetaris, George A. and Betty A. Dobratz, "An Empirical Test of Gordon's Ethclass Hypothesis Among Three Ethnoreligious Groups", *Sociology and Social Research,* 61:39—51. Oct., 1976.

Kramer, Judity R. and Seymour Leventman, *Children of the Guilded Ghetto.* New Haven: Yale University Press, 1961.

Laumann, Edward O., *Bonds of Pluralism.* New York: John Wiley and Sons, 1973.

Lazerwitz, Bernard and Louis Rowitz, "The Three-Generation Hypothesis", *American Journal of Sociology,* 69:529—538. Mar., 1964.

Lenski, Gerhard, *The Religious Factor.* Garden City, New York: Anchor Books, 1963.

—————————, "The Religious Factor Revisited", *American Sociological Review,* 36:48—50. Feb., 1971.

Lerner, Michael, "Respectable Bigotry", *The American Scholar,* 38:606—617. Aug., 1969.

Levine, Irving M. and Judith Herman, "The Life of White Ethnics: Toward More Effective Working-Class Strategies", *Dissent,* 19:286—294. Winter, 1972.

Levy, Mark R. and Michael S. Kramer, *The Ethnic Factor.* New York: Simon and Schuster, 1972.

Liberson, Stanley, "A Societal Theory of Race and Ethnic Relations", *American Sociological Review,* 26:902—910. Dec., 1961.

—————————, "Stratification and Ethnic Groups", *Sociological Inquiry,* 40:172—181. Spring, 1970.

—————————, *Language and Ethnic Relations in Canada.* New York: John Wiley and Sons, 1970.

Light, Ivan, *Ethnic Enterprises in America.* New York: World, 1972.

Lipari, Marie, "The Padrone System", *Italy-America Monthly,* 2:4—10. Apr., 1935.

Lopreato, Joseph, "Upward Social Mobility and Political Orientation", *American Sociological Review,* 32:586—592. Aug., 1967.

—————————, *Italian Americans.* New York: Random House, 1970.

Mangione, Jerry, *Mount Allegro.* Boston: Houghton Mifflin, 1942.

McLaughlin, Yans, "Patterns of Work and Family Organization: Buffalo's Italians, *Journal of Social History,* 5:299—314. Fall, 1971.

Michelson, William, *Man and His Urban Environment.* Reading, Massachusetts: Addison-Wesley, 1970.

Mindel, Charles H. and Robert W. Habenstein, *Ethnic Families in America.* New York: Elsevier, 1976.

Monticelli, S.F., "Italian Emigration: Basic Characteristics and Trends with Special Reference to Post-War Years". In *The Italian Experience in the United States.* Edited by S.M. Tomasi and M.H. Engel. Staten Island: Center for Migration Studies, 1970. Pp. 3—22.

Muraskin, William, "The Moral Basis of a Backward Sociologist: Edward Banfield, The Italians, and the Italian-Americans", *American Journal of Sociology,* 79:1484—1496. May, 1974.

Nelli, Humbert S., "Italians in Urban America". In *The Italian Experience in the United States.* Edited by S.M. Tomasi and M.H. Engel. Staten Island: Center for Migration Studies, 1970. Pp. 77—107.

Nelsen, Hart M. and H. David Allen, "Ethnicity, Americanization and Religious Attendance", *American Journal of Sociology,* 79:906—922. Jan., 1974.

Newman, William M., *American Pluralism: A Study of Minority Groups and Social Theory.* New York: Harper and Row, 1973.

Nie, Norman, *etal. Statistical Package for the Social Sciences.* New York: McGraw-Hill. 1975.

Noel, Donald L., "A Theory of the Origin of Ethnic Stratification", *Social Problems,* 16:157—172. Fall, 1968.

Novak, Michael, *The Rise of the Unmeltable Ethnics.* New York: Macmillan, 1971.

Parenti, Michael, "Ethnic Politics and the Persistence of Ethnic Identification", *American Political Science Review,* 61:717—726. Sept., 1967.

Rosenthal, Erich, "Acculturation Without Assimilation: The Jewish Community of Chicago", *American Journal of Sociology,* 66:275—288. Nov., 1960.

Rossi, Peter, "Review of 'The Urban Villagers' ", *American Journal of Sociology,* 70:381—382. Nov., 1964.

Rossi, Peter H. and Alice S., "Some Effects of Parochial School Education in America", *Daedalus,* 90:300—328. Spring, 1961.

Russo, Nicholas J., "Three Generations of Italians in New York City: Their Religious Acculturation", *International Migration Review,* 3:3—17. Spring, 1969.

Sandberg, Neil, *Ethnic Identity and Assimilation: The Polish Community.* New York: Praeger, 1973.

Sartorio, Enrico, *Social and Religious Life of Italians in America.* Clifton, New Jersey: Augustus M. Kelley, 1974.
(Originally published in Boston: Christopher Publishing House, 1918.)

Schermerhorn, Richard, *These Our People.* Boston: D.C. Heath and Company, 1949.

_____, *Comparative Ethnic Relations: A Framework for Theory and Research.* New York: Random House, 1969.

Shibutani, Tomatsu and Kian M. Kwan, *Ethnic Stratification.* New York: Macmillan, 1965.

Silverman, Sydel. "Agricultural Organization. Social Structure, and Values in Italy: Amoral Familism Reconsidered". *American Anthropologist,* 70:1-20. Feb., 1968.

Spiro, Melford E., "The Acculturation of American Ethnic Groups", *American Anthropologist,* 57:1240—1252. Dec., 1955.

Steinberg, Stephen, *The Academic Melting Pot.* New York: McGraw Hill, 1974.

Stonequist, Everett V., *The Marginal Man.* New York: Charles Scribner's Sons, 1937.

Strodtbeck, Fred L., "Family Interaction. Values and Achievement". In *Talent and Society*. Edited by D.C. McClelland, *etal*. Princeton: D. Van Nostrand, 1958. Pp. 135—194.

Suttles, Gerald D., *The Social Order of the Slum*. Chicago: University of Chicago Press, 1968.

——————————, *The Social Construction of Communities*. Chicago: University of Chicago Press, 1972.

Thomas, John L., "The Factor of Religion in the Selection of Marriage Mates", *American Sociological Review*, 16:487—491. Aug., 1951.

Tomasi, Lydio F. *The Italian American Family*. Staten Island, New York: Center for Migration Studies. Spring, 1972.

Tomasi, Silvano, *Piety and Power*. Staten Island: Center for Migration Studies, 1975.

Turner, Frederick Jackson, *The Frontier in American History*. New York: Henry Holt and Company, 1920.

Vecoli, Rudolf. "Prelates and Peasants: Italian Immigrants and the Catholic Church". *Journal of Social History*. 2:217-268. Spring, 1969.

——————————, "Born Italian: Color Me Red, White and Green". In *The Rediscovery of Ethnicity*. Edited by Sallie TeSelle. New York: Harper and Row, 1973.

Vickery, William E. and Stewart G. Cole. *Intercultural Education in American Schools*. New York and London: Harper and Brothers. 1943.

Warner, W. Lloyd and Leo Srole. *The Social Systems of American Ethnic Groups*. New Haven: Yale University Press. 1945.

Weber, Max, "The Ethnic Group". In *Theories of Society*. Vol. 1. Edited by Talcott Parsons. Glencoe, Illinois: The Free press, 1961.

Wheeler, Thomas, *The Immigrant Experience*. New York: The Dial Press, 1971.

Whythe, William Foote. *Street Corner Society*. Chicago: The University of Chicago Press. 1943.

Wilensky, Harold L., "Mass Society and Mass Culture", *American Sociological Review*, 29:173—197. Apr., 1964.

Williams, Phyllis H., *Southern Italian Folkways in Europe and America*. New Haven: Yale University Press, 1938.

Winch, Robert F., Scott Greer and Rae Lesser Blumberg, "Ethnicity and Extended Familism in an Upper-Middle Class Suburb", *American Sociological Review*, 32:265—272. Apr., 1967.

Wolfinger, Raymond E., "The Development and Persistence of Ethnic Voting", *American Political Science Review*, 59:896—908. Dec., 1965.

Wrong, Dennis, "How Important Is Social Class?". In *The World of the Blue-Collar Worker*. Edited by Irving Howe. New York: Quadrangle, 1973. Pp. 297—309.

Yancey, William L., Eugene P. Ericksen and Richard N. Juliani, "Emergent Ethnicity: A Review and Reformation", *American Sociological Review*, 41:391—403. June, 1976.

Yinger, Milton J., *Sociology Looks at Religion*. New York: Macmillan, 1963.

Zangwill, Israel, *The Melting Pot*. New York: The Macmillan Company, 1909.

INDEX

ETHNICITY AND MIGRATION SERIES